THE UNEXPECTED!

Okee was not at all like a dog or a cat. A dog or a cat can be left alone to amuse itself. Not an otter! Okee had to be part of everything I was doing. If I was sweeping, he had to ride on the broom; if I was ironing, he had to hang on the cord; if I was washing the floor, he had to sit on the sponge or play in the water; if I was careless enough to walk past him with a full bucket of water, he would sneak up behind me and tip the bucket. Scolding Okee for being naughty did no good. I soon learned that an otter never learns the meaning of the word no. To an otter, *no* means stop for a minute and begin again as soon as the coast is clear....

THE TRUE STORY OF OKEE THE OTTER
was originally published by
Farrar, Straus & Giroux, Inc.

Critics' Corner:

"When the author (a librarian) and her husband decide to adopt an otter as a household pet (previous wild boarders included an owl, two bats and a groundhog), her library friends hold a surprise baby shower —harbinger of the book's friendly informality. At first, the Wisbeskis fear for Okee's (for Okefenokee) loss of freedom, but the Columbian otter proves he can improvise in suburban New Jersey, sometimes to the couple's chagrin. Chasing a runaway otter through a sewer is not the way to spend a quiet evening at home.... Okee manages to pick every lock in the house, plays magician with every cloth and doily, and learning to paint, appears with his 'Ot' work in a New York store. This report of life with an unusual pet offers the fun without the fuss, and the appealing home photographs are a good match for the personal tone."

—*The Kirkus Reviews*

"The book abounds with Okee-created hilarity told with humor and understanding. But also, it successfully makes known the ways of an otter in a human environment, the difficulties and hazards to be faced in successfully rearing one and keeping it healthy."

—*Defenders of Wildlife News*

About the Author:

DOROTHY WISBESKI is one of those gifted people who have a special way with animals. When she was a child, she coaxed birds to feed from her hand, and in third grade she beat up the class bully—a boy larger than herself—for mistreating a cat. The children's room in the Bound Brook (N.J.) Memorial Library, of which Mrs. Wisbeski is in charge, at one time included forty-three parakeets, a catfish, two tanks of tropical fish, two guinea pigs, mice, turtles, hamsters, and frogs—until more space had to be made for books.

THE TRUE STORY OF OKEE THE OTTER

Dorothy Wisbeski

ILLUSTRATED WITH PHOTOGRAPHS

AN ARCHWAY PAPERBACK

WASHINGTON SQUARE PRESS • NEW YORK

THE TRUE STORY OF OKEE THE OTTER

An Archway Paperback edition

1st printing....................September, 1969

2nd printing.......................August, 1970

L

Published by Washington Square Press,
a division of Simon & Schuster, Inc., 630 Fifth Avenue, New York, N.Y.

WASHINGTON SQUARE PRESS editions are distributed in the
U.S. by Simon & Schuster, Inc., 630 Fifth Avenue, New
York, N.Y. 10020 and in Canada by Simon & Schuster
of Canada, Ltd., Richmond Hill, Ontario, Canada.

Standard Book Number: 671-29281-1.
Library of Congress Catalog Card Number: 67-25679.

To my husband
Luke
who managed to keep his sanity
even with an otter in the house

He prayeth well who loveth well
Both man and bird and beast.
He prayeth best who loveth best
All things both great and small;
For the dear God who loveth us,
He made and loveth all.

SAMUEL TAYLOR COLERIDGE

THE
TRUE STORY
OF
OKEE THE OTTER

1

Okee's story began on April 30, 1962. It was not his birthday. In fact, he wasn't even born yet. This was the day I sent a special-delivery letter to a New York pet shop. The letter said:

Dear Sir:
I would like to order a baby female otter. Enclosed you will find a deposit of $25. I will pay the rest when the otter arrives.

Sincerely yours,
Dorothy Wisbeski

Thus began six long weeks of waiting.

I had liked otters for a long time. Many times I had seen them in the zoo. How playful they were, always swimming, jumping, sliding, and doing tricks! A happy-go-lucky animal like that seemed just right for our active household. My husband, Luke, and I had raised many wild animals in the past—an owl, a starling, some robins, a bat, two skunks, mice, turtles, squirrels, an opossum, and even a groundhog. The groundhog, our favorite of all, had just died early in April, after living with us for five years. Because we missed her so much, we knew we must have another wild animal to replace her.

We were not afraid now to take on an animal we knew little about. Our many experiences had taught us that love, patience, and understanding can tame a wild animal. Surely an otter would be no different. I would soon find out, however, that an otter is not like any other animal in the whole world.

Since the otter was to be my pet, it was up to me to decide before she arrived where she would sleep, swim, and play. This was easier said than done, for our small house with its medium-size yard seemed crowded already.

2

Trouper, Luke's huge German shepherd dog, stayed in the kitchen during the night and in the side yard during the day. Pierre, my parakeet, lived in the bedroom. The basement was used for laundry, storage, and Luke's carpenter shop. If Luke and I were to keep the living room for ourselves, that left no place for the otter except in our new tiled bathroom. It would be fine while the otter was small, but I knew an active animal could not live in it long. Oh, well, I thought, I'll worry about that when the time comes.

Because we live on a busy corner and have no fence around our yard, I knew it would not be safe for the otter to be free outside. That didn't mean she could never go out. There is a small park across the street, and a canal and woods nearby. These would be perfect places to take an otter for a walk. As for a swimming place for her, I had that all figured out too. Luke is very clever at building. I was sure he could build an enclosed pool with a sliding board that would make any otter happy.

Word traveled fast in the library where I work. Before long, hundreds of children and adults knew about my expected otter. To the children who came to my library, waiting for the otter was like waiting for the arrival of a new baby brother or sister. Hardly a day went by that they did not inquire about the otter. They began to get very interested in all otters, and read everything they could find about them. When I wasn't busy, they asked me to tell them what I had learned about otters. I'm afraid it wasn't much, for very little had been written about pet otters.

Some of my little library friends even planned a surprise for me and our otter-to-be. When I arrived at the library one Saturday morning early in June, there were no children in sight. This was unusual, for on Saturday they are always there first to greet me. Even Elaine, one of the teenage girls who worked for me as a page, was missing. How strange everything should be so quiet! I thought no more about it for a while and concentrated on getting my room ready for the day.

I was so busy I only half noticed the steady stream of children sneaking into the staff room behind the children's room. Half an hour went by, and I was just about to look for Elaine, my missing page, when suddenly she appeared in the doorway of the back room. She looked very worried as she called for me to come. Something terrible must have happened, I thought as I hurried to her. As I got closer, I became aware of hushed giggles coming from behind the closed door. The instant I opened it, I was greeted with a loud shout of "Surprise!" The smiling, freshly scoured faces lined up behind the table told me at once that the surprise was a party.

I still did not know the reason for the party. I glanced around the room hoping for a clue. There were balloons, mostly pink ones, everywhere. They hung from the ceiling. They stuck to the walls. They were all over the counter, all over the refrigerator, and even in the icing of the beautifully decorated cakes in the center of the table. I peeked at the cakes—no clue there. All that was written on them was "Best Wishes," in pink. The entire room was decorated in pink—pink crepe paper, pink tablecloth, pink dishes, pink napkins. Even the presents lying about were wrapped in pink and white paper with pink ribbon. But I didn't guess what it all meant until the children explained. The party was a baby shower for my expected girl otter!

To children, the most important part of a party is the food, so I waited until every child had had his fill of cake, ice cream, cookies, nuts, potato chips, and soda. Then I began to open the presents. In the first package was a pink harness, decorated with shiny studs and jingle bells. I was pleased to see that the children had purchased the one-piece, figure-eight type. This is the best kind of harness for an animal that has no distinct neck. The other presents were chosen with the same care. There was a rubber frog for her bath, because frogs are a natural part of an otter's diet. There were two rubber penguins and a duck, because they, too, live in water. Marsha, the little girl who had planned the party, gave the most original gift. It was a painting called "Bird of Paradise." She had made it especially for the otter's room.

For all the pleasure they had given me, the children asked only one thing in return. They wanted to help me choose a name for the otter. I had thought of many: Ophelia, Olivia, Olympia, Oleo, Octavia; but the name I kept coming back to was OKEFENOKEE. It is an Indian word meaning "trembling earth," but that is not why I like it. Many years ago I saw a film of the wildlife found in the great Okefenokee Swamp in southern Georgia. The name fascinated me, and so did the otters in the film. I told the children about it, and they all agreed that this would be a perfect name for the otter. For easier calling, we would shorten it to Okee.

On the following Monday, I went to work feeling very happy. It was a beautiful June day. Somehow I had the feeling I was going to receive good news. I was right. Late that afternoon, Mr. Hermann from the pet shop called me. He told me that a baby female otter had been found in Colombia, South America. She would be placed on a jet plane leaving South America on Wednesday. Should all go well, she would arrive at Kennedy Airport in New York on Thursday. A veterinarian would meet her at the plane and give her a mild serum to protect her from enteritis. I was pleased to hear this. Enteritis is a disease that kills many baby otters. Mr. Hermann told me he would call again tomorrow to let me know when the otter would be delivered. When I said goodbye, I knew I would hardly be able to wait until tomorrow.

Sure enough, Mr. Hermann called me the next day as he had promised. The otter had arrived safely and would be delivered by station wagon to our house in New Jersey the next day.

I had so many questions to ask, I couldn't get them out fast enough. How old was she? How big was she? What color was she? What was I to feed her?

Mr. Hermann answered all my questions patiently. He told me she was about five weeks old, weighed only three pounds, and was about ten inches long, including her tail. She was a beautiful dark chocolate-brown color.

Because she was so young, she would have to be put on a special feeding formula for a while. Mr. Hermann suggested Esbilac, a milk formula made especially for animals. He assured me she would be ready to eat solid food in about three weeks. When she was full grown, he said, she would weigh no more than fifteen to nineteen pounds and would probably eat a pound and a half of fish daily.

Since she came from a tropical country, he warned I must not let her get chilled.

It almost sounds too easy, I thought, as I hung up the phone.

2

As a rule, I sleep late on my day off, but there was no sleeping late that day. There was too much to do to get ready for Okee. Her formula had to be mixed and poured into sterilized bottles. Water to be mixed with her cereal and with syrup for in-between feedings had to be boiled. All dishes and pans which she would use had to be sterilized. The tiled bathroom which was to be her nursery would need to be thoroughly scrubbed with disinfectant. I was taking this animal away from its natural home. It was up to me to keep it happy, safe, and comfortable. Household germs would be new to this animal from the wild. The fewer germs there were, the less chance there was of her becoming sick.

For the time being, her bed would be a cardboard box lined with soft pink blankets. I had raised enough baby animals to know how important it was to keep her warm and dry. A kitty-litter pan, the kind indoor cats are trained to use, had already been purchased. It needed only to be filled with fresh clean wood shavings to make it ready for use. I hoped Okee could be trained to use such a pan.

We worked hard all that day, scrubbing and scouring. Morning passed; afternoon came and went. Night came and still the otter had not arrived.

By 10 P.M., Luke and I were feeling quite discouraged. Mr. Hermann had phoned in the afternoon and assured me the otter had left New York with the delivery man at 10 A.M. Where were they all this time? Could it be that they weren't coming at all? I gave one last look out the window. Just as I did, a dark green station wagon rounded the corner and stopped under the street light in front of our house. A short, stocky man bounced out of the car, carrying a small, dark furry form

11

nestled in the crook of his arm. In an instant I was at the door.

"Here's your otter," the man said. The next moment I was holding the softest, most adorable animal I had ever seen. Okee had arrived at last!

She was sound asleep and perfectly limp, but she woke as soon as I carried her into the house. I was so busy getting acquainted with her I had a hard time listening as Frank, the delivery man, gave us his final advice: "Make sure her food is always fresh. If you have any problems, call Joe Davis at the Bronx Zoo, and remember you'll have to teach her how to swim."

Teach her how to swim? I don't even know how to swim myself, I thought, as we thanked him and said goodbye.

After Frank left, I hurried to the kitchen to warm a bottle of formula for Okee. My, how hungry she was! The milk just wouldn't come out fast enough for her. She hung on to the bottle tightly with her front paws and made loud sucking noises as she drank.

After her meal, we had a chance to examine her more closely. We measured her length with a tape measure. From the tip of her nose to the tip of her tail she was exactly twelve inches. Her chocolate-brown fur shone like the coat of a seal. We stroked her gently. She felt as soft as velvet. Her eyes were round and the same color as her fur. They seemed to dance like a clown's eyes. Her round face with its many whiskers made me think of a catfish. A big yawn revealed a mouthful of tiny pointed teeth.

By this time, our dog, Trouper, was aware there was a stranger in the house. At first we were afraid to let them meet. Trouper was so used to sharing his house with other animals that he accepted each new arrival without fuss. But we did not want the otter to become frightened on her first night in our house. It might spoil any future friendship. Trouper begged so hard to be allowed to visit the new baby that we finally took him into the living room for a brief look. Poor Trouper! All he did was take one sniff at the little dark blob in the center of the floor and the little blob tottered to its feet. Before Trouper could back away, the little animal lashed out and bit him right on the end of his very sensitive nose.

In spite of this bad beginning, they soon

became very good friends. A little later, Okee was taking a between-feedings nap on a rocking chair in the living room. Trouper seated himself on the floor in front of the rocker, staring at the bundle that never moved. Trouper never moved either. Only his ears twitched once in a while when he caught some faint sound coming from the chair. He looked just like a father watching over his sleeping child. I'm sure he felt he was guarding her.

Okee slept well during the night, but I didn't. Early in the morning I was awakened by a terrible smell coming from the otter's box. The books I read about otters said their coats have a heavy doggy odor, but this did not smell like a dog. It smelled like a skunk who had just fired his "musk gun." I knew that all members of the weasel family were equipped with "musk guns," which they fire when they become frightened. Somehow, I didn't expect the otter to smell worse than its cousin, the skunk. Unlike skunk musk, however, otter musk disappears in about twenty minutes. This fact, together with a little scented spray, soon took care of the problem.

Okee's first day with us was a busy one. She had to be fed every two hours and exercised every three. By mid-morning we figured out she had a definite schedule of her own. She would be awake for fifteen minutes, then asleep for an hour. When she was sleeping, nothing could disturb her.

She was in just such a deep sleep that afternoon when we took her to the veterinarian for her first checkup. Though the doctor twisted her, turned her, and rolled her over several times, she did not wake up during the entire examination. The doctor found nothing wrong, but he suggested that we bring her back in ten days for another checkup.

The next few days, we seemed to spend most of our time feeding Okee and taking her visiting. We wanted her to meet as many people as possible while she was young. We hoped then she would not fear humans when she grew older. To become tame, any kind of wild animal must be treated with kindness from the time it is a baby. Okee was certainly getting her share of fondling, and we could see she loved it.

By the end of the first week, Okee was eating eight meals a day of milk, cereal, and vitamins. She was now strong enough to walk, but we couldn't help laughing at her when she did. Her walk was a comical flat-footed, humpbacked, ducklike waddle. It was hard to believe that this awkward, potbellied baby would some day become a graceful, beautiful animal.

After ten days she was still healthy, and we felt very proud. Just to be sure, though, we took her to the vet's for her second checkup. It was not as easy to examine her this time. She had become very ticklish. Each time the doctor put the stethoscope on her chest, she wiggled. When he tried to examine her stomach, she burped. When he tried to look down her throat, she tried to grab his nose. She was so lively I found it hard to believe the doctor when he told us her temperature was 104 degrees and her right lung was badly infected. Unless he gave her a penicillin injection right away, there was great danger she might die from pneumonia.

We already knew that otters can get sick very quickly, but we knew they can get better quickly too. We left the office knowing that by the next day she would either be getting better or she might be dead.

Okee did not die. The medicine helped her at once, and in three days she was almost completely well. But this didn't mean our worries were over.

Feeding now suddenly became a problem. Instead of taking her milk greedily as she used to, Okee would chew the rubber ends off the bottles and let the milk spill out all over the floor. No amount of coaxing would make her accept her bottle again. We were beginning to find out that otters can be very, very stubborn, a trait they never lose.

We mixed the milk with her cereal and tried force-feeding her with a spoon. Luke usually held her and I aimed the spoon. I think wrestling an alligator would have been easier. Okee refused to open her mouth.

There was nothing left to do but try some other food. Otters are supposed to like fish, so we tried that next. At the first whiff she made a funny face; at the second, she shook her head, and at the third she ran away. Hamburger was our next choice, and Okee loved it. But it upset her stomach. One by one, we tried different foods with the raw hamburger. After two weeks we finally found a formula to suit her. It was a raw meat loaf made up of

17

cereal grains, egg yolk, wheat germ, bone meal, powdered milk, and vitamins. We fed this to Okee in little meatballs, one at a time. She never grabbed for the food, no matter how hungry she was. She would open her mouth, put her head back, and then rock back and forth like a trained seal waiting for a fish. Unlike a seal who gulps his food, she chewed hers thoroughly.

By the time we took Okee to the vet for the next checkup, she was livelier than ever. Her weight had increased from three and a half pounds to seven and a half pounds. She was very strong, and the vet told us she was completely well.

He told us something else too. Someone had made a mistake. Our otter was not a girl but a *boy!*

3

*I*t didn't take us long to learn that Okee made a game out of everything. And it didn't take our otter long to learn that water games are the most fun of all.

It all began when we gave him his first drinking dish, a large clay bowl. We tried to keep it filled with water, but Okee didn't like the water in the bowl. He would rather have it in puddles all over the floor. Then he could slap it with his paw and make drops hit the ceiling, or pretend to swim through it.

He would dive into each fresh bowl of water, dunking his whole head all the way up to his ears. As soon as his nose reached the bottom, he would turn over and do a back bend. He practiced this trick every day. Soon he was able to do the dive and flip-over so fast he could make a big wave of water slosh right out of the bowl. Then he would fall in the puddle of water on purpose just to make it splash all over the walls.

Every day Okee invented more water tricks. From headstands and back bends he went on to handstands and leapfrogs. It wasn't long before he found out how he could get wetter faster. He would pick up the bowl with his front paws and dump the water all over himself. Though Okee's front paws were partly webbed, he could use them like hands.

Okee's swimming lessons began the day I took away his small bowl and gave him a large deep dish. It was large enough to get his whole body into, except for his long tail. But Okee soon learned what to do with his tail. He would back up to the dish and put his tail in the water first. Then he would roll over and sit on his tail.

When Okee outgrew the dish, we gave him a dishpan. When he outgrew the first dishpan, we gave him another. He grew out of pans faster than children grow out of shoes.

Meanwhile, I was getting very tired of mopping up. During the day, when I was at work at the library, we left Okee safely locked in the bathroom. Many times I wished that my tiled bathroom had a drain in the floor. Each day when I came home, I found the floor covered with water.

By now, many of the children in the neighborhood had heard about the swimming lessons and came to watch. What an actor Okee was! He just loved to show off. The more people there were watching him, the better the performance.

The children squealed with delight at his tricks. Sometimes he would float on his back with his head underwater. Other times he would bend his body like a pretzel and then do corkscrew rolls. His body seemed to be made of soft rubber. He did hoop rolls and back bends, and even tried a few dives off the edge of the pan. Dives were always sure to cause a big laugh when the waves splashed out of the pan and into some child's lap.

After a while the front row learned to wear raincoats.

Okee even made a game out of the drying that followed the swim. The object of the game on my part was to dry him. The object of the game on his part was to keep from being dried. Drying an otter is not easy. First, you have to be fast enough to catch him. Then, you have to be strong enough to hold him down and keep him from wiggling. If I got his head in the towel, his tail stuck out. If I got his tail in the towel, his head stuck out. It would have been easier to dry an eel or an octopus. After about five minutes and three towels, Okee would be dry and I would be wet. If I forgot to pick up the pan of water right away, he would jump back into it. Of course, this meant we would have to start the whole routine all over again.

When I was home during the day, Okee usually had four swims. (For each one I used fresh towels, and it took quite a few towels to dry Okee, for otter fur soaks up water like a sponge.) At the end of the day I would hang out all the wet things to dry. People who saw my clothesline must have thought I had twenty children or more. If this kept up, I knew I would need to buy a washer and dryer just to do Okee's laundry.

As the weather grew warmer, Okee wanted to be in and out of water all day. Luke and I agreed. It was time for Okee to learn to swim in the bathtub. For the first few days I put only a few inches of water in the bathtub. Each day I put in a little bit more. I was afraid Okee would get frightened if the water was too deep too soon. Okee liked to lie on his back in the tub under the faucet. He would gurgle with delight as the stream of water hit him on the chest.

One day I left him in the tub with the water running slowly, and took a walk outside. I planned to go back in a few minutes and turn the water off. But I forgot. I became so interested in my flower garden that fifteen minutes went by before I remembered what I had done. Oh, dear, I thought! The tub must be filled by this time. I ran into the house trembling to think what I might find. I knew Okee couldn't get out of the tub, for I had locked the shower doors. I was sure I would find Okee drowned.

But I didn't! The tub was filled to overflowing, but there, going back and forth

upside down, was Okee. He'd never had a
real lesson, but he was swimming like a fish,
and diving, too. Just to show off, he did a
couple of back flips off the edge of the tub.
There was no need to worry about Okee
drowning after this. Whenever I wanted a few
minutes' peace, I would fill the tub and let
him go swimming.

My, how he loved the tub! Before long, he
could hold his breath for several minutes underwater. He could swim with his tail or his
hind foot in his mouth. He could even put all
his feet in his mouth and sit on the bottom of
the tub. Many people find it hard to float, but
for Okee it was easy. He could even float
while balancing a ball and his rubber goldfish
on his stomach. His diving improved too.
After a week, he was able to dive to the
bottom of the tub with a ball tucked under
each arm and a toy between his hind feet. In
such cases he didn't use his feet at all to
swim. It was the swishing of his strong mus-
cular tail that made him move.

Okee was not satisfied just to splash in the
tub. He had to make waves. By swimming
back and forth across the tub very fast, he
would make the water rock. Then he would

lie on his back and let the waves sway him back and forth. The bigger and stronger he became, the higher the waves he could make. Luke made a special clamp which he put on the outside of the shower doors to keep them shut so otter and water would stay in the tub. It was a good thing he did. By the end of the summer, Okee was riding waves up the sides of the tub and even eight inches up the walls. He didn't need a surfboard. He had his own built in.

Whenever I had a free moment, I enjoyed watching Okee play in the tub. He didn't need fancy store-bought toys. He could have just as much fun with an old peach pit. His games were played by definite rules which he made up himself. First, he would swim back and forth across the tub with the pit balanced on his nose. Then he would flip over on his back and catch the pit on the palm of his paw. While holding the paw with the pit on it above the water, he would use his other three legs to push himself around the tub. The object of the game was to complete the trip around the tub without dropping the pit.

When Okee tired of his balancing game, he would push the pit up the side of the tub with his nose. When he got it there, he would knock the pit off with one paw and catch it in the other. If I sat on the floor by the tub, he would swim over to me with the pit in his mouth. With a look that said, "Please," he would beg me to play with him. If I held my hand out, he would lean over the tub and drop the pit in my hand. Then he would back off and wait for me to throw it. Before the pit had a chance to hit the bottom of the tub, Okee would swim under it and catch it on his nose. With the pit balanced on his nose, he would swim over to me and then push it up onto the edge of the tub. That was a signal to start the game all over again.

If Okee didn't have a peach pit, an empty gallon plastic bleach bottle could keep him just as amused. Try as he might, he couldn't sink the bottle. If he draped his whole body over his bottle raft, he could submerge it a few inches. Oh, how he loved to slide off the bottle and hear it go "POP" as it exploded to the surface!

Okee seemed to enjoy playing tricks on the people who came to watch him swim. If the people laughed, Okee would remember the tricks and do them again and again. One such trick was squirting people with water, not with a water pistol, but with his rubber penguin. He would squeeze the penguin until he forced all the air out of it. Then, he would take it down to the bottom of the tub until it filled up with water. After that, he would come to the surface and very slyly put the penguin on the edge of the tub.

As soon as someone bent over the tub to get a better look at him, Okee would leap up out of the water and pounce on the penguin. WHAM! He would slap it hard with both paws. For an otter, Okee had excellent aim. He usually got his poor victim square in the face.

Okee had use of the tub so often Luke and I had to wait until late at night for our baths. Taking a bath was no longer a simple matter. Before the water could be put in the tub, we had to remove rubber toys, ping-pong balls, bottle caps, wads of paper, and peach pits. Next the ring of dirt that Okee always left in the tub had to be removed. If we were lucky, there might be a dry towel or two left for us. Often we were not that lucky. But then, that's life with an otter!

4

My vacation time had arrived at last. I had been looking forward to it ever since Okee came. It was going to be a time when I could rest and quietly enjoy my otter. That's what I thought, but Okee saw to it there was no time to relax. Every minute he was awake, he expected my complete attention. Early each morning he began to demand his breakfast long before I was ready to get up.

When we were home in the evenings and on weekends, Okee had the run of the house. But to make sure he was safe while we slept, we locked him in the bathroom at bedtime.

He didn't seem to mind while it was dark, but as soon as morning came he let us know he wanted out. First he would rattle the door. By lying on his back on the floor, he could get a good grip on the bottom of the door. Then, by pulling back and forth as hard as he could, he could produce a terrible racket. It was so awful, it usually made Luke spring right out of bed as if he were shot from a cannon. By the time Luke got to the door and unlocked it, Okee would be back in his box, sucking his foot and pretending to be asleep to escape the spanking he sometimes got for making noise early in the morning.

Luke would hardly be back in bed when Okee would be up again, this time throwing his toys around. BANG! A plastic whiffle ball would hit the ceiling. CRASH! His drinking bowl would hit the wall. PING! PING! Two jelly beans would hit the shower doors. It sounded as if he were a whole team playing basketball, football, and baseball all at the same time.

If we managed to stand the noise, Trouper couldn't. The bangs and the crashes would soon set him to barking. The more the dog barked, the more noise the otter made. SQUEAK! would go Okee's rubber duck as he squeezed it with his paws. BLUB! would go the rubber frog as he sat on it. This was more than poor Trouper could take. He would start howling at the top of his voice, going up and down the scale like an opera singer practicing her notes. There was no use trying to sleep once Trouper started to sing. We might as well get up and start entertaining Okee.

Okee was not at all like a dog or a cat. A dog or a cat can be left alone to amuse itself. Not an otter! Okee had to be part of everything I was doing. If I was sweeping, he had to ride on the broom; if I was ironing, he had to hang on the cord; if I was washing the floor, he had to sit on the sponge or play in the water; if I was careless enough to walk past him with a full bucket of water, he would sneak up behind me and tip the bucket. Scolding Okee for being naughty did no good. I soon learned that an otter never learns the meaning of the word no. To an otter, *no* means stop for a minute and begin again as soon as the coast is clear.

There were many little extra jobs around the house I planned to do during my vacation. And I might have done them, too, if Okee had not kept me so busy. It was during my vacation, for instance, that Okee learned to climb stairs. At first he would grab hold of the carpet on the stairs with his front paws and pull the rest of his body up. He would do this one step at a time. Sometimes he would lose his grip before his hind end reached the step and he would tumble backward down the stairs. He was always so relaxed he never hurt himself when he fell.

Coming down was another matter. He would simply relax, throw himself forward, and flow down the stairs. His limp body would take the shape of every step as he flowed over it. His movements looked like a snake's, only they were much faster. In the same way, he flowed over the edge of the sofa, over the seats of the chairs, and over my lap and down my legs. Eventually his hind legs grew strong enough to support his weight. Then he could get up and down the stairs by making comical flat-footed rabbit hops.

Since he could now move around so well, I

kept a careful watch on Okee. However, he still managed to vanish once in a while. I was really worried the night he disappeared for twenty minutes. It was quite a surprise to find him outside on the front porch. Luke had gone outside shortly before and had left the front door ajar. Curious Okee had discovered the door was not tightly closed and pushed his way out. Then the wind slammed the door shut and Okee could not get back inside. He became frightened and started to chirp and scratch until we found him. Now that Okee knew about doors, we would have to make sure they were always locked. Okee's memory was amazing. He would never forget how he got outside.

From the very beginning of his training, Okee had enjoyed the out-of-doors. We tried to plan our time so he would have some out-of-doors play each day. He could not be left alone outside, for he would chase anything that moved—leaves, bits of paper, birds, and even cars. Many a time we would have to run after him and make a flying tackle as he dashed off into the street after a car or a bicycle. After a summer of running and tackling, Luke and I would have made good football players. People walking by fascinated Okee too, and he would follow anyone who looked friendly.

Okee loved to go for a walk. He started taking hikes around the park every day when he was a baby. He knew his harness meant he was going for a walk, so as soon as he saw it being taken from the cabinet drawer, he ran to the back door. He spread himself out flat on his stomach and waited for Luke to place the harness across his back. At the words, "Roll over," he turned over on his back. Luke then fastened the harness under his stomach. Once he was ready, Okee chattered impatiently, as if he were telling us to hurry up.

Wild otters are supposed to be very clumsy and awkward on land, but Okee was not. Daily practice soon taught him to walk easily. The skin on the soles of his feet became so thick it did not hurt him to walk over rough sidewalks or cinder roads. The muscles in his back and legs grew very strong, and he soon could trot along for half a mile without stopping. By autumn, he would be able to walk as far as two miles if he rested once in a while.

I was often busy with housework, so it was

usually Luke who took Okee for his walks. Okee loved Luke so much he would follow him on a walk just like an obedient dog. Unless Luke planned to cross a busy street, he didn't even have to attach a leash to Okee's harness. When Okee stopped to rest, he would always lay his chin on the top of Luke's shoe. No one else's shoe would do. How comical he looked when he walked fast. He was pigeon-toed in the front, flat-footed in the rear, and hump-backed in the middle. The faster he walked, the higher he held his tail, but it was too long and heavy to curl it up over his back as many dogs do. When Okee dragged his tail along the ground, we knew we was getting tired.

Often his daily walk would come after a summer shower. When it did, Okee was delighted. He would wade through every puddle and slosh through every patch of mud along the way. From the very first time Okee met mud, he loved it. At home, if there wasn't any ready-made mud, Okee would make his own. He knew there was always a pan of water and soft dirt in Trouper's pen. Whenever Okee was turned loose in the yard, he would scramble under the gate to Trouper's pen and upset the dog's water. Then he would lie down on his chest in the mud he just made, and belly-whop all around the pen. He didn't need a hill. He had merely to tuck his front feet at his sides, hunch his back, and push himself with his hind legs.

Next to hiking and playing in mud, Okee's favorite outdoor sport was chasing Trouper around the yard. Okee's short legs made him no match for long-legged Trouper, but that didn't stop him. He didn't seem to care whether or not he won the race. Trouper would pass him four times before Okee finished one trip around the house. Still, Okee would keep running, humping his back up and down, like a speedy inchworm. If his small plastic pool was out in the yard, Okee would often take a quick dip in it while the race was going on. He could dive into the pool and out the other side without even stopping.

Trouper might have been faster than Okee, but Okee was smarter. He knew how to catch Trouper if he really wanted to. For the first few trips around the house, Okee would run behind the dog. Then suddenly Okee would turn around and run in the opposite direction. Before the surprised dog knew what happened, the otter would meet him head on.

Okee loved riding in a car and went for a ride in our station wagon almost every day. When he was tiny, I used to hold him in my arms. When he got a little bigger and squirmier, Luke invented an otter car seat for him, using a cardboard box. He fastened a leash to each side of Okee's figure-eight harness. Then he tied the two ends to the sides of the box.

Okee's first trips in the car were short ones. He went to the bank, to the supermarket, to the post office, and to the library. We often took Trouper along to act as baby sitter. Several times a week we took them to busy shopping centers. This was all part of our plan to get Okee used to people and noise. If we wanted to shop, we never had to worry about leaving Okee in the car. Trouper saw to it that no one got near the otter. But Okee saw to it that Trouper got no rest. He would chew on the dog's feet, tail, and ears until the dog was worn out. When Luke thought the dog had enough, he would take them both for a walk outside while I shopped inside.

Walking about with a pony-size dog and an otter was sure to attract attention. Luke didn't mind the crowds that followed him. Nor did he mind answering the many questions people asked, but Trouper watched the crowd carefully. If anyone gave Okee too hard a pat, he would growl and push the offender aside.

Okee and Trouper were now inseparable. Each night, Trouper would challenge Okee to a playful wrestling match on the living-room rug. To someone who didn't know they were friends, their matches looked like fierce battles. Okee's loose-fitting tough hide kept him from getting hurt by the dog's teeth. His skin seemed to be attached to his body in only six places—four feet, nose, and tail. Everywhere else it hung like a wrinkled sack, or a suit that was too big.

The dog didn't get hurt either, for his long bushy coat protected his tender skin from Okee's sharp teeth. Trouper would often grab Okee by the head and try to drag him around like a football. Okee knew exactly what to do to make Trouper let go. He would turn in his own skin and grab the dog's tender tongue. If he grabbed too hard, Okee's four very sharp canine teeth would sometimes leave holes in the dog's tongue. Trouper would cry out in great pain, but he would never bite his little friend.

If Trouper was lucky enough to catch the otter on his back, he could pin him to the floor by standing on his loose skin. It didn't take Okee long to figure a way out of that predicament. He would start wiggling like a worm on a hook until Trouper's foot started to slip. Quicker than the time it takes to say "Okefenokee," he would be free. Before the dog realized what was happening, Okee would wriggle rapidly backward under Trouper's belly, come up behind the dog, grab his tail, and hang on. This would so surprise the dog that he would take off through the house like a jet-propelled plane, with Okee hanging on behind.

Though I loved Okee dearly, it was Luke whom Okee loved best. Okee showed affection to me only when Luke was not at home. Then he would allow me to pick him up and cuddle him, but never for very long. If I managed to hold on to him for fifteen or twenty seconds, that was a long time. Okee just couldn't be still for any longer than that.

During the brief time that I held him, Okee would investigate every inch of my face. He would look up my nose, in my eyes, and then poke his nose into my ears. It seemed as if he were trying to figure out what made me tick. At the end of the examination, he would wrap his paws around my neck and nip the end of my ear with sharp otter teeth. Being loved by an otter turned out to be a painful experience.

Okee had to have his rough and tumble play every day, and that could be painful, too. I know Okee didn't really mean to bite or hurt us. I guess he thought our skin was as tough as his hide. By the end of the summer, however, my arms and legs were covered with black, blue, and yellow bruises. The way people looked at me when I went out, I was afraid they thought Luke was mistreating me. From then on, whenever Okee was in a playful mood, I wore heavy leather gloves to protect my hands.

My vacation had been anything but restful. Four weeks of constant otter-sitting had left me feeling limp. I was actually looking forward to going back to work. My busiest day at the library couldn't be half as busy as a day with Okee. The last four weeks made me realize that as long as Okee lived in my house I would never have a day when I could do exactly as I wanted. Okee had not lost his freedom by coming to live with me. I had lost mine!

5

*O*kee continued to grow at the rate of one pound and one inch each week. By the time he was three months old, he had outgrown his cardboard-box car seat. We tried keeping him on a leash in the car, with me as an anchor. But he was so big and strong I could no longer hold him still. A fifteen-minute ride with him had me exhausted, while poor Luke would be hanging on to the steering wheel, trying desperately to see the road through dangling otter feet and tail. I knew the time had come to put Okee in a cage when we traveled, but I hated to think of locking him up behind bars. He loved his freedom so much I was sure he would not be happy in a cage, even for a little while. It was Luke who made the final decision. Better to have Okee in a cage than risk having an accident on a busy road.

Luke started building Okee's cage the next day. It was a large, comfortable-looking cage with a wooden floor and heavy wire sides. To make sure there would be plenty of ventilation, we made the top also of wire. It seemed sturdy enough to hold a lion, but I had some doubt in my mind whether it would hold an otter. Okee had already amazed me with his super-strength. To prevent his playing in the toilet bowl at home, I had always weighted down the lid with a twenty-two-pound rock. Though he now weighed only ten pounds, he had recently learned to push the rock up with his nose and slip under the lid. I wondered how long it would take him to push his way out of Luke's otterproof cage.

Okee's first big adventure in his cage was on a trip to a state park sixty-five miles away. I had a feeling we would need extra help on this trip, so Mimi, one of my helpers from the library, was invited to go along. To test the cage, Okee was placed in it an hour before we started out. I expected him to fly into a rage, but he didn't. When a few head butts against the top and sides of the cage did not break the wire, he gave up. I could not understand it. It was not like Okee to give up without a fight. Instead of having his usual temper tantrum, he lay down on his back and cried. How sad he looked lying there with tears streaming down his cheeks! His shrill "Chirrup, chirrup," told us how hurt he felt. I wanted to let him out, but I knew if I did I would never get him used to his cage.

Mimi and I tried our best to console Okee, but nothing we did helped. He chirped, and screamed, and cried for almost the entire sixty-five miles. When we finally reached the park, we all had headaches. Even Trouper acted as if he couldn't stand another minute with all that noise. Once Okee was set free in the park, he changed his voice to chuckling grunts. These were happy sounds. They seemed to say, "What a relief to be free again! Thank you very much."

There were so many things to carry for our hike in the park I was glad that Mimi was along to help. She had Okee's towels in one hand, a thermos jug filled with Okee's water in the other, the camera bag across one shoulder, and Okee's thermal bag filled with hamburger across the other. I carried the movie camera and held on to Okee on the end of a twelve-foot leash. Luke carried our lunches and held on to Trouper's leash. Walking along the edge of the lake, one after the other, we looked like an African hunting party.

From time to time Okee would dive into the lake and swim out to the end of his leather lead. Then he would disappear under the water. Trouper, no doubt, thought Okee was drowning. Each time Okee swam out more than a few feet from shore, Trouper would dive in and pull him out by the scruff of the neck. Okee finally gave up the thought of swimming and was satisfied to play in the mud along the shore.

Quite by accident, Okee invented a game along the hike. It was such fun, from then on, he played it every time we took him for a walk. When he was tired, he had a habit of lying down flat on his stomach and refusing to move. If he was tired enough, he would even take a little nap. Usually I would wait for Okee to get up on his feet before starting out again. But this time he was lying on a patch of soft wet grass. I wondered what he would do if I pulled him. He couldn't get hurt, so I decided to try it.

At first, Okee put on his rear "brakes" by digging his heels down into the grass and dirt. Then, for some reason, he decided to try the ride. He lay down flat on his stomach, tucked his front legs at his sides, stretched his hind legs out behind him, and relaxed. It was just like pulling a sled through snow. Okee really seemed to like this kind of tobogganing. For the rest of the hike, whenever we came to a wet grassy patch Okee would lie down and wait for me to pull him.

Okee had behaved badly enough on his way to the park, but for part of the trip home he was even worse. He banged his head against the wire of the cage, scratched at the floor, tore his blanket to shreds, and screamed until he was exhausted. When he could scream no more, he collapsed into a sound sleep. Tucked under his right arm was his favorite traveling toy, the rubber duck the children from the library had given him some months before.

It was several weeks before we tried another long trip with Okee. By this time, he was used to his cage and no longer cried when he had to ride in it. Traveling in the dark sometimes frightened him, though. When he couldn't see us, he would stick his paws through the wire of the cage, hoping to feel one of us. I found I could comfort him by holding his paw. With his paw in my hand I guess he felt safe, for he would soon fall asleep. If we traveled in daylight, he often amused himself by playing with his toes or by juggling his toys on his feet. Juggling was easy for an animal whose hind feet were shaped like small snowshoes.

Okee was only four months old when we took our first trip to the seashore with him. One hundred and twenty-eight miles was a long ride for such a young animal. To make matters worse, it was a very hot day. This meant we had to plan carefully to keep Okee cool. We knew that if his body got too hot he would faint and perhaps even die. To be sure this didn't happen, we took along fifteen gallons of cold water in thermos jugs and bottles. The water was for Okee to swim in and drink along the way. A metal dishpan would serve as a bathtub. A large bag of ice cubes was added to the equipment. Should Okee get very, very hot along the way, we would cool him off by dunking him in a pan full of ice cubes.

Our planning was not in vain. Several times along the way, Okee's body got dangerously hot. He panted so hard we thought surely he was going to pass out. We would let him slosh around in some water in his pan then, and that cooled him off enough so we could drive on. If Okee was just slightly warm, we could cool him off by wrapping him in wet towels for a few minutes. Letting him play with ice cubes in his cage was another way to keep his body temperature down. Okee liked it when I placed five or six ice cubes on top of the cage and let them drip down over him. He would roll over on his back and try to catch the drops on his front paws. Sometimes he would let the drops bounce off his nose and then catch them in his mouth. That was Okee—making a game of everything!

Three and a half hours after our start, we arrived at the beach. To get from the car to a place where we could let the animals swim, we had to walk more than a mile. For easier walking, we kept to the wet, hard-packed sand along the edge of the water. Okee refused to let me carry him. Whenever he got tired, he waded into the surf and swam. It amazed me to see that he could dog-paddle as fast as we could walk.

We had to parade in front of thousands of bathers to get to our swimming place. A huge dog and an otter cannot walk along the beach without attracting a great deal of attention. Before long, we found ourselves being followed. The line of people behind us grew longer and longer as we walked along. Word had spread that we were going to let Okee swim in the ocean. An otter swimming at a public beach was a rare event. No one wanted to miss it.

At last we reached the spot where Okee was to try his first swim in deep water. The water was calm when we started out, but suddenly it became very rough. Several times Okee was knocked over by large waves, but with Luke close by, he was not afraid. He learned to dive under breakers three or four feet high as they thundered into shore. When the wave passed, he would come up in almost the same place he went down. With a little coaxing, he was soon diving from Luke's shoulders.

If Luke moved more than a few feet away, however, Okee would panic. Bubbling and spurting like a motorboat, he would paddle frantically to reach Luke's side. This fear of being left alone in strange water stayed with Okee even when he reached adulthood. If he were left free to swim in a river or a pond, he never went far from shore. He would stay in the water only as long as he could hear or see Luke.

Once Okee became used to the water, we turned Trouper loose to play with him. How Trouper worried about Okee! If he felt Okee was out too far, he would swim out after him, grab him by the back of the neck, and drag him back to shore. But in a few seconds Okee would be merrily out to sea again with Trouper in hot pursuit. When Trouper made a grab for him, Okee would dive down about three feet, swim swiftly under the dog, and come up behind him. The poor dog would flounder around in circles while Okee dipped and dived over, under, and around him, moving as easily and as gracefully as a playing porpoise.

When Okee grew tired of teasing Trouper, he took hold of the dog's tail with his paws and his mouth and let the dog tow him to shore. Even Trouper seemed to enjoy the applause and cheers from the watching crowd. It was a rare treat to see an otter and a dog playing in the surf. Hundreds of people would never forget it.

Okee's adventure at the shore tired him out, so he went right to bed when we arrived home. In fact, he was so tired he didn't wake up for fourteen hours. This was the first time since Okee arrived that Luke and I were able to enjoy a quiet evening together. How strange it felt not to have a noisy otter tearing the house apart.

6

*I*t was early August. Okee had come through the most dangerous part of his babyhood, but I wondered what the next few months would bring. When I stopped to think how little we knew about otters, it amazed me that we had done so well. There were no books written on the care of otters in captivity. We had to guess at what was best for Okee. Okee was healthy now, but I wondered if he would stay that way without his natural diet of fish.

My mind was full of questions. He was born in Colombia, South America, which is a very hot country. Would he be able to adjust to New Jersey's cold wet winters? When he became an adult, would he turn wild, as so many captive animals do?

As I thought about all of this, I suddenly remembered what Frank, the delivery man, had said the night he brought Okee to our house. "If you have any questions, call Joe Davis at the Bronx Zoo." Thinking that Joe Davis was probably a zoo keeper in the otter pen, I decided to call him. Imagine my surprise when I learned he was not a keeper but the Curator of Mammals. He was responsible for seeing to it that all the mammals in the entire zoo were properly cared for. It was a big job. I would not have bothered him with my phone call if I had known how busy a man he was.

Mr. Davis was not annoyed at my call. Instead, he was very pleased. He told me he had bought an otter for himself just three weeks before, and he had heard that I owned one just like it. Since my otter was a month older than his, he was interested in knowing how I had managed to keep it alive. No one knew better than he how quickly infant otters can die. The year before, enteritis had killed two baby otters he was trying to raise as pets.

Also, the zoo's baby otter that had been shipped with Okee had died a short time after its arrival. Mr. Davis felt we had a better chance to keep both our otters alive if we shared what we learned about them.

That was the beginning of a whole series of telephone calls between Mr. Davis and me over the next two months. Like two mothers comparing their children, we compared our otters. Mr. Davis called his otter Beever because it looked a little like a real beaver and the name was easy to say. Both otters had weighed three pounds when they arrived. By the middle of August, Okee weighed ten and a half pounds. Beever, who was also gaining a pound a week, weighed six and a half pounds.

The markings on both otters were the same —three yellowish-orange patches of fur, one on the underside of the neck, one on the chest, and a large one on the stomach. I learned later that only Colombian river otters have these marks. The rest of the coloring was the same on both otters. They were dark chocolate brown on top and silver brown underneath. In sunlight, the outside, or guard hairs, took on a silver sheen. Under artificial light, the shiny fur took on the colors of the rainbow, much the way a soap bubble does.

Their noses were jet black and shaped like rounded triangles with the point on top. Mr. Davis explained that different kinds of otters have different-shaped noses. He said zoologists can tell one kind of otter from another by looking at its nose. Beever and Okee had round flat faces instead of long slender faces like the Canadian otters I had seen at the zoo. Both had stout bodies and four webbed feet. Both were still teething, but Okee, because he was older, had already started with his molars. Unlike many animals whose back teeth are blunt, otters have molars that are sharply pointed.

By the third or fourth telephone call, Mr. Davis and I felt like old friends. We dropped the formal "Mr." and "Mrs." for Joe and Dotty. As Mr. Davis said, two people "nutty" enough to choose to live with an otter ought to be friends. I felt better knowing Joe was always ready to help if Okee needed it. It made him feel good, too, to know that I was willing to help him if he had problems with Beever.

We always spent a good deal of time talking about feeding problems. Okee, while not yet four months old, was already eating a pound of food a day. This was as much as an adult otter eats, according to the animal books I had read. Yet otters are not full grown until they are two years old. I told Joe that if Okee's appetite continued to increase, by the time he was two he might be eating ten pounds of food a day!

Both otters were on the same hamburger formula, but by the end of September each developed a fondness for something extra. For Okee it was chicken, carrots, potato peelings, orange skins, grapes, baloney, ice cream, Jello, and rubber bands. Joe reported that Beever's tastes were much more expensive. For a side dish, he liked avocados and cheese. These extra foods were given only once in a while, however. We did not want to spoil our otters' appetites for the balanced diet they needed each day.

Joe used to worry about the fact that the otters did not have fish in their diet. Then he learned there were other pet otters, much older than ours, who also would not eat fish. Like Beever and Okee, they were fed meat, cereal grains, and vitamins. Joe guessed that pet otters refuse fish because they were captured so young their mothers did not have time to train them to hunt. I'm not sure how Joe felt about it, but I was glad that Okee had never been taught to kill.

Beever's appetite was never as large as Okee's. Because Okee had someone around to play with him most of the time, he was very active. Beever never got as much playtime as Okee, because Joe's job at the zoo kept him away from home for such long periods of time. Also, Beever never learned to accept strangers. But Okee enjoyed rough-house play, not only with us and Trouper, but with Mimi and others who came to otter-sit, and with children who visited him.

It isn't hard then to understand why Okee needed six meals a day to keep him going, while Beever needed only three. Okee's constant exercise and his extra meals made him much bigger and stronger than Beever. When Okee could climb and jump three feet high, Beever could only reach six inches. After hearing about all the things Okee reached and broke, Joe said he was very happy that Beever had never learned to climb well.

The more I talked to Joe, the more curious I became about him. I wondered what he was like. Was he young or middle-aged? Was he tall or short, fat or thin? By the end of October, my curiosity got the better of me and I invited us to Joe's house. "I'd be glad to have you come," he said, "if you don't mind being bit." He explained that Beever didn't like strangers and growled at them.

Two days later, we were on our way to Joe's house. It was only sixty-three miles away, so we decided to take Okee with us. I was sure Joe would want to see him as much as I wanted to see Beever, even though we agreed we wouldn't try to introduce the otters to each other unless Beever seemed friendly.

Joe was not at all the way we thought he would be. He seemed so young for such an important job at our country's largest zoo. Instead of the bald head I thought he would have, he had lots of dark brown hair cut in a crew cut. With his dark-rimmed glasses, he looked just like a studious college boy. Luke expected to find him dressed in a business suit. Imagine Luke's surprise when Joe greeted us at the door dressed in old pants with one knee torn, a sweatshirt, and heavy leather boots. His outfit wasn't fancy, but he certainly did look comfortable.

Joe warned me not to expect a tidy house, so I really wasn't surprised to find things scattered all over. I could excuse Joe, though. He lived alone. His otter and fennec (desert fox) kept him so busy there was little time left for housework. Besides, very few men enjoy doing housework. Books and papers were stacked on the living-room chairs. Joe's typewriter was on the dining-room chair. Some artwork he was doing for a magazine covered the dining-room table. On the counter tops in the kitchen were packages and bottles of food for Beever's formula. I wondered where Joe ate his meals, but I didn't ask. Perhaps he ate standing up.

I could see Joe had made changes in his house for Beever. His bed was equipped with special metal legs to raise it three feet off the floor. At this height, Beever couldn't climb into it. Everywhere I looked, there were barriers of cinder blocks and plywood. They were put up to keep curious little paws out of electrical sockets and appliances. The beautiful fireplace in the living room was boarded up to prevent the disappearance of a little otter up the chimney. Soaps and poisonous cleaners were hidden away out of reach in high places.

After a brief tour of Joe's little house, we sat down in the living room to talk. By this time Beever, who had been sleeping when we arrived, knew there were strangers in his house. His natural otter curiosity made him come out to investigate. We could hear him growling as he came. This was a new sound to us. Okee had never growled. He didn't need to. He had seen so many people since babyhood he learned to love them all.

Beever refused to make friends. He growled most of the evening. Several times he crept under the sofa where we were sitting. With a warning "Ha," he jumped at our feet as if he meant to bite us. His attacks turned out to be bluffs. I guess in his own otter way he was telling us to go home. Joe thought Beever was too upset to take a chance on a meeting between him and Okee. I was quite sure Okee would be friendly, but Joe was just as sure Beever would not.

After the first hour, Beever calmed down enough to let us watch him swim in his tub.

Beever's tub looked like Okee's with its assortment of toys—whiffle balls, rubber squeak toys, etc. In water, Beever was a typical otter, carefree, happy, and full of play. Like Okee, he enjoyed doing stunts with much swishing and splashing. He didn't splash quite as much as Okee, though. I guess it was because Okee had so many more baths a day than Beever. He had much more time to learn fancy tricks.

I noticed that Beever was just as smart as Okee in figuring out how to let the water out of the tub. Okee could undo or pull off any kind of wires or snaps that Luke put on the drain lever to keep it shut. Luke would spend hours working out these inventions. How stupid he felt when it took Okee only a few minutes to have the water gurgling down the drain again. Like Okee, Beever enjoyed playing with the whirlpool that formed at the drain as the water went down. I guess otters behave like otters no matter where they live.

We had been telling Joe all evening how gentle and friendly Okee was. To prove it, we now invited Joe out to the car to meet Okee. When Joe saw how large our otter was, he wasn't so sure he really wanted to meet him. However, he climbed in, sat down in the front seat, and waited for Okee to come out of his cage.

In a matter of seconds, Okee was beside Joe, sniffing at his coat pocket. I could see Joe stiffen as Okee came near. Joe knew enough about otters to know how hard they can bite if they want to.

"Pick him up, Joe," Luke said. "He won't bite you."

Joe didn't move. Okee never gave him a chance. He crawled into Joe's lap and wrapped both paws around Joe's neck. While Joe sat there quite surprised, Okee looked in his eyes, in his ears, and in his nose. Okee even accepted food gently from Joe's hand, just as we said he would. Our big, lovable otter had proved we were right.

I knew Joe loved Beever too much to give him up ever. It was quite a compliment to Okee, though, when Joe said as we left, "Do you want to trade otters?"

7

*F*rom the day of his arrival, Okee, it seemed, was the most important member of our household. Luke used to joke about it. "Okee's not our pet," he would say. "We're his."

In a way, that was true. Most of our time was spent trying to find out what Okee liked or needed or wanted. And Okee had many ways of letting us know how he felt about things.

For the first few weeks Okee lived with us, he made no sounds. He didn't need to. He spoke with his eyes. When he was hungry, he would sit in front of the refrigerator and stare at the door. It was almost as if he expected some kind of magic to open the gate to hamburger heaven. When he was thirsty, he stood up in front of the sink and stared at the faucets. When his eyes drooped sadly or became glassy, we knew at once that he wasn't feeling well. How hurt he could look when he was scolded for being naughty, and how charming he could look when he wanted to be forgiven! "I didn't mean to hurt you," his eyes would say when he got a slap across the tail for nipping an ankle too hard. Like a child, when he was tired it showed in his eyes. But when he was happy his eyes seemed to sparkle and dance with merriment.

There were some things Okee did that made him take on an expression of sheer delight. No child making mud pies could look happier than Okee making patty-cakes in a dish of ice cream. If I happened to leave a bowl of Jello on the kitchen table, and left the room, it was certain Okee would find it. He loved to sit in the middle of the table and toss lumps of soggy Jello over his shoulder. My expression was anything but happy when I sat on a chair smeared with sticky ice cream, or stepped in blobs of Jello Okee had thrown down the cellar steps.

If we watched Okee carefully enough, we could usually tell by his devilish expression when he was thinking of doing something naughty. Most of Okee's mischievous pranks he decided upon on the spur of the moment. When he rolled his eyes, opened his mouth, and grinned, I knew something was about to happen at once. In the next second or two I could expect to find Okee swinging on the hanging lamp above my bed or wallowing in the dirt from a spilled flower pot. If he got away with these pranks, I might expect to see him running off with my shoe, which of course he would soak in the toilet. Perhaps next I would hear a bag of potatoes bouncing down the cellar steps. There seemed to be no end to the amount of mischief he could create in one evening.

Once Okee's voice developed, he could let us know by sounds what he wanted. The sound heard most often was a low-pitched oinking grunt, spoken very rapidly. It had several meanings. Okee grunted as he trotted along behind Luke on a walk as if to say, "I'm coming." In the morning or after a long time away from us, it meant, "Hello. I'm glad to see you. Where have you been?" Sometimes it was a coaxing sound. Spoken in front of the refrigerator, it meant, "Please feed me." In front of the closed shower doors, it meant, "Please open the doors. I want to go swimming." Grunting at the back door meant "Please, may I go out?" and in the living room it meant "Come play with me."

It was a happy grunt when someone he liked came to visit him. First he would sniff the visitors. Starting with the feet first, he would work up to their faces. Okee would stand up on his hind feet and stretch as high as he could. Looking up into the visitor's face, he would grunt, "Uh, uh, uh, uh, uh." In this case the grunting meant, "Please bend over so I can see you better." Most people who came to visit did as Okee asked. As soon as they bent over, Okee would press his face against theirs and grunt softly. As nearly as I can figure out, he was saying in otter talk, "Open your mouth." For some reason he liked to peer down people's throats. He looked for all the world like a doctor examining someone's tonsils. Joe Davis thought that perhaps he was smelling people's breaths so he would know them the next time they came.

When Okee asked for something and we didn't give it to him quickly enough, the grunting sounds would change to chirping chatter. The sound was something like a scolding chipmunk's or a squirrel's, only much louder. "Open the door," the chattering seemed to say, when he was locked out of a room. The longer he had to wait, the louder and more shrill the chirps became. "Hurry up!" his voice said. "I've had enough of this nonsense. Open this door at once!" He grew more annoyed by the minute and his voice took on a threatening tone that was part growl, part scream: "Open this door or I'll break it down." Then he pounded, scratched, and pushed. I could stand the chirps, but when he scraped his nails on the linoleum, the sound made shivers run up and down my spine. That did it! I opened the door.

Sometimes his oinks of pleasure turned to grumbling oinks. When we were out visiting, this sound meant, "I'm getting tired. Let's go home." Hiccups were added to the grumbles if we didn't start for home at once. When Okee lay on his back and grumbled, chirped, and hiccuped, it meant he was getting very, very, impatient.

Okee could not see very well at a distance. He depended on his excellent hearing to tell him when someone was coming near. Sometimes he would be so interested in what he was doing, he would not hear me when I came up behind him. "Ha!" he would say when I came close enough for him to see me. In this case it meant, "Oh, you frightened me." One "ha" was a sound of surprise, but a double, "ha, ha," was a warning to keep away.

Okee "ha'ed" at anything new that came into the house. A new rug or piece of furniture, a large box, a hat, an unfamiliar coat were all approached cautiously and "ha'ed" at. If they didn't "ha" back, they were accepted. We sometimes used this "ha" when we wanted Okee to stand still for a picture. If we "ha'ed" at him when he was doing something naughty, he would stop for a few moments. Okee was too clever, though, to be fooled often. This trick was successful only if we used it once in a while.

We could tell by watching Okee's mouth

whether he was sad or happy. If he got a spanking, that made him sad, and the corners of his mouth turned down. If something he did made him very happy, the corners of his mouth would turn up. With his round face, his sparkling eyes, and his three-corner nose, he looked just like a smiling jack-o'-lantern. Okee smiled when he wriggled and rolled on the living-room rug, and he smiled when he played games he made up himself. But his biggest smiles came when he was in a tub of water.

Once Okee learned to turn the shower on, he delighted in dancing under the spray. As the water poured down on him, he would stand up on his hind feet and waltz round and round the tub. When he made an extra-fancy turn, he held his mouth open in a big half circle. If it is possible for an otter to grin, then Okee was certainly doing it.

There were times when Okee could make his voice sound like chuckling laughter. When he smiled and chuckled at the same time, he was the perfect picture of a laughing otter. We found that Okee's chuckles came only when he was the happiest. He chuckled when he was being dried after his bath; he chuckled when he was being tickled on the stomach; and he chuckled when his harness was being strapped on him for his walk outside.

Okee was only five months old when I heard those chuckling noises for the first time. He was in the tub with the water running slowly. I was in the kitchen making my lunch. All of a sudden, I heard the water come on full force. No doubt Okee had turned the faucet knob. He had done this many times before. But, smart as he was, Okee had not learned to tell the difference between the hot and cold faucts. I rushed to the bathroom to make sure he wasn't scalding himself. Sure enough, he had turned on the hot water. Since the shower doors were locked, there was no way for him to escape.

As fast as I could, I removed the clamps that held the doors shut. Then I leaned across the tub to turn off the water. The next thing I knew, my feet slipped out from under me on the wet floor. Before I could stop myself, I landed head first in the tub.

To this day, I can see Okee as he was when I stood up dripping wet. His front paws were propped on the sides of the tub. His head was tilted back and cocked to one side. Showing through his whiskers I imagined I saw a faint grin. All the while he looked at me, I could hear him making loud chuckling noises.

Somehow I could not help but feel my little otter was laughing at me.

8

Okee was only a little more than six months old when he discovered a way to reach the faucets in the bathroom sink. The sink was too high for him to reach standing up. However, there was a stool in the room near the bathtub. Otters aren't supposed to climb, but Okee didn't know that. He had learned to climb very well. One day Okee pushed the stool over to the sink and climbed up on it. Now he could reach the faucets without even stretching. It didn't take him long to learn how to turn them on.

Of course, he never bothered to turn them

off. He had no reason to. Okee didn't care if my bathroom floated away. To an otter, nothing is as much fun as running water, so he just let it run. He also enjoyed soaking things in water. Day after day I would come home from work to find my towels soaking in a sinkful of water. On the floor would be another inch of water, and soaking in that would be yards and yards of toilet tissue.

Something had to be done. I could no longer keep Okee locked in the bathroom during the day. Being locked alone in a small room for five or six hours was more than Okee could endure. He was bored, and when an otter is bored, he gets into trouble. He not only turned on the faucets, he also pulled down the curtains, tore the window shade, and ate the fringe off my rug. I had to move Okee. The basement was the only place in the house large enough and sturdy enough to hold an otter. From then on, Okee's home was in the basement. He was allowed upstairs only when there was someone at home to watch him.

I was afraid Okee would be unhappy all alone in a dark basement, but he wasn't. There were so many places to explore and so many different things to see he had no trouble keeping himself amused. He pried apart cabinet doors and pulled open all the drawers he could find. Whatever was in the cabinets or drawers, he pulled out on the floor. He so completely emptied everything that he found things we had been looking for for months. When Okee finished taking them apart, they might as well have stayed lost. He found my galoshes and chewed the toes out of them. He found a bundle of bills Luke had lost almost a year ago. After he chewed the papers to bits, it would have taken Luke another year to put the pieces back together again. Luke's missing rubber gloves turned up too, without their fingers, of course!

We never knew what kind of mess we would find when we came home from work. One day Okee found a box of soap powder hidden back in the corner of a cabinet. He didn't need to read the directions on the box to know what to do with it. He chewed the top off the box and dumped the contents on the floor. Soap powder is no good dry, so he set out to get some water. The closest water was in the basement toilet. He soaked himself in the bowl. When he was thoroughly wet, he rolled in the soap powder. The water from his fur mixed with the powder, making a sticky paste which was just delightful for sliding. All around the cellar floor he went, leaving a trail of soap slides behind him.

Okee's favorite place in the cellar was the toilet bowl. It was everything an otter could hope for. It was a place to get a drink, a pool to swim in, and a puddle to play in with toys. At first we tried to discourage him from this kind of play. But no matter how Luke would weight down the toilet lid with rocks and pieces of iron, all Okee had to do was wedge his nose under the lid and lift. Luke even tried tying the weights down with heavy ropes and many knots. But by the time we got home from work Okee would have the ropes untied. There in the toilet bowl would be Okee's treasures—his rubber penguins, half a rubber ball, bits of wood and paper, and nails stolen from Luke's workbench.

Luke finally gave up. He cleaned the bowl out thoroughly, disinfected it, and said from then on it would be only for Okee.

Okee liked having his own private pool, even if it was a bit too small for swimming.

He invented all kinds of games to play in it. A favorite game was trying to push things down the drain. Once, it took Luke three days to unplug the pipe after Okee jammed a large onion down the drain. But that was only a small problem. Our big problem began when Okee learned how to flush the toilet.

At first, Okee flushed the toilet only when he wanted fresh water to drink, or to swim in. Then, when he grew so large he could no longer fit his whole body in the toilet bowl, he flushed it to make a pool on the floor. As the water came pouring out from the tank, Okee would jump in the bowl head first. This caused the drain to stop up and water would spill over onto the floor. Over and over he would flush the toilet. Soon he would have a pool on the floor large enough and deep enough to keep him happy for hours.

At this point, Luke suggested filling the laundry tub with water. Perhaps then Okee wouldn't need to make such large pools on the floor. With an otter you have to be willing to try anything. There is no way of knowing what he will like or not like. This time Luke's idea worked. From his first dip, Okee was delighted with his new tub pool. Even when he grew so large he had to double himself in two to fit into it, he still swam in the tub every day. He seemed happier than he had ever been before. To see him happy made me happy.

Giving Okee the laundry tub to swim in still didn't keep him completely out of mischief. More water meant he had more room to soak things. Until Luke put a lock on the hamper, we used to come home nights and find our laundry soaking in the tub. When Okee could no longer get to the laundry, he raided Luke's workbench. There were so many drawers to open and explore he could keep himself busy for hours, just pulling things out. Everything he could cart away he soaked in his tub. Hammers, saws, pliers, rulers, screwdrivers, and planes were dropped, dragged, or pushed into the tub. It was amazing how he could manage to swim with a tub full of tools.

For a while, nothing serious happened in our house. Little things were always getting broken or ruined by water, but Luke and I were used to the small, everyday damages. They seemed to go with an otter. But every so often Okee would do something that would try our patience to the very limit. It was times like this when we realized how important it was to love Okee whether he was good or bad. Too many people have animals destroyed or shipped off to a zoo if they cause trouble or make extra work. Okee made me angry at times, but I never once thought of sending him away.

If ever I had good reason to give Okee away, it was the night he got out of the basement while we were away. We hadn't planned to be gone long that evening, so we did not hire an otter-sitter. Elaine or one of the other girls who were Okee's friends sometimes came and played with him when we went out for an entire evening. But this time luck was against us. We missed our bus and then had car trouble, so we were away for three hours longer than we expected.

We had known for some time that Okee knew how to open the door between the kitchen and the cellar by turning the doorknob. We had seen him many times jump up and grab the knob with his front paws. Then he would pull his body up off the floor until his chin rested on the doorknob. All he had to do to turn the knob was to wiggle his body. Now that he knew how to turn the knob, we kept him in the basement by locking the door on the kitchen side with a key. For some reason, when we left that night, each of us thought the other had locked the door. Neither of us went back to check. Since Okee had had his supper and some playtime before we left, we were not too worried about being late.

It was 11 P.M. when we arrived home. I expected to walk into the tidy house I had left a few hours before. But when I turned on the light, everywhere I looked there was something turned over, crumpled, or broken. At first sight, I thought our house had been ransacked by burglars. Then I spotted a trail of water that led from the bathroom through the kitchen, across the living room rug, and into the bedroom. Now I knew who the guilty one was. Burglars who had come to rob a house would not have stopped to take a bath!

Okee must have worked very hard to have made such a terrible mess in such a short time. There was very little he had missed. The bookcase had been emptied, and the books were lying in heaps on the floor. The bed pillows were stuffed behind the rocking chair in the living room. The floor lamps were leaning cockeyed against the walls. The bathroom towels were jammed in the toilet, along with two erasers from my desk drawer. Luke's sandals were crammed in a bottom bureau drawer. White socks were hanging out of the drawers like so many icicles from a roof. The legs of all the kitchen furniture were wrapped with one long ribbon of blue toilet tissue. The bathroom light was on, the exhaust fan was buzzing merrily, and the heater was blasting like fury.

If Okee had just upset things, it wouldn't have been so bad, but he didn't stop there. When I recovered from the first shock, I took a closer look. I nearly fainted at what I saw. Okee had painted my entire house with mud. There were mud pictures all over the walls, the floor, the stove, the sink, the rugs, the cabinets, the woodwork, the curtains, and the bedspreads. But where did Okee get the mud? The trail of water leading from the bathtub to the plant stand in the bedroom gave the answer. He had opened the shower doors and had taken a dip in the tub. While he was dripping wet, he had climbed up on the plant stand and upset seven potted plants. A thoroughly wet otter mixed well with seven potfuls of dry dirt could produce nothing else but mud. On my rug was a large brown stain—all that was left of Okee's gigantic mud pie. Okee didn't need art lessons to know what to do with the mud. Any otter knows that mud is delightful, and the more it is spread around, the more fun it is.

It seems funny to me now as I write about it, but it wasn't funny then. As I stood in the center of the living room looking at the damage in all directions, I'm not sure whether I felt sick or angry. I began to think what I would do to Okee when I found him. For a brief second I imagined him as an otter fur coat, but in the next second I hated myself for such a thought.

It didn't take long to find Okee. As I stepped into the bedroom, the mattress on Luke's bed suddenly moved away from the wall. Popping up from behind it, like a hand puppet, was one slightly damp otter. All but his face was wrapped in a mud-splattered bedspread. If I was expecting him to look sorry for what he had done, I was disappointed. Peering through the fringe which fell across his face were two round otter eyes. They were alive with excitement and merriment. Across his whiskered face was a big happy smile. His expression seemed to say, "I guess I got even with you. See what happened because you stayed away so long!"

I wanted to give Okee a good sound spanking and would have if Luke hadn't rescued him. Luke knew how angry I was. He thought it best if he took Okee out of the house and left me alone to calm down. As quickly as he could, Luke rounded up all the muddy rugs, towels, and bedding and then packed Okee and Trouper into the car. Luke spent the next three hours in the Laundromat doing the wash.

Luke was even kind enough to forget to say what he had said so many times before. Whenever I complained about Okee's behavior, Luke's answer always was: "You wanted an otter!"

This time, even without Luke saying them, the words kept repeating themselves in my mind. And as I calmed down I knew Luke was right. Whatever troubles I had with Okee I had brought on myself. Okee had not chosen to live with me; I had chosen him.

9

Christmas was always a lively time in our
house. This year I had a feeling there would
be more excitement than usual. Keeping an
active otter out of a Christmas tree was
going to be a real challenge. We always made
our own decorations for the tree, but what
kind could we make that an otter couldn't
destroy? The only truly otterproof ornament
would have to be of rock or iron. I thought
about it for days and then an idea came to
me. Why not use Styrofoam balls? They were
cheap, light in weight, and easy to decorate. I
figured the tree would hold two hundred. To

allow for otter "accidents," I bought four hundred.

One month before Christmas, I started decorating the Styrofoam balls for the tree. Since I always like my tree to be different from everyone else's, I decided to make the little round balls look like the heads of people I knew. I made a teacher, a lawyer, a farmer, a nurse, and a policeman. Soon Luke became so interested he decided to make some little people too. A day later, Okee joined the craft project, uninvited, of course. It didn't matter to Okee whether we wanted him or not. His mind was made up. When an otter makes up his mind to do something, no one changes it.

With the addition of four curious paws, the project began meeting with "accidents." Because there was no other table large enough, we had to work at the kitchen table. Okee always sat at the table to eat his meals, so he regarded it as partly his. For a while, he would sit on his chair and swat whatever came close to him. If one of the Styrofoam balls happened to roll near, he would pick it up in his mouth and run and hide it.

Okee was clever enough not to do anything

naughty while I was watching him. He was also smart enough to know when I was so busy with craftwork that I wasn't paying any attention to him. That was the time he chose to dip his paws into the box of sequins. By the time Luke and I realized what he was doing, there were sequins all over the table, the floor, the chair, and Okee. To make a grab for him when he had his feet in the box was a big mistake. Okee would shift his feet to the edge of the box and dump it. Ten thousand sequins would spill all over the floor.

If it wasn't sequins he was putting his paws in, it was glue. Otters just have to feel everything with their paws. Okee found that by dumping the glue on the table he could get both paws wetter faster. As long as the glue was wet, Okee enjoyed pushing it around on the table. When it started to dry on his paws, and he couldn't lick it off, he would panic. He would thrash around wildly. By the time we caught him, everything near him would be stuck up too. While Luke held him down, I put glue thinner on his paws to remove the glue. Okee was so fond of the smell and the feel of glue that even the thought of getting stuck up didn't keep him away for long.

With two people working on them, it didn't take long to make fifty heads. The kitchen table was no longer a safe place to keep them. Okee had discovered what fun it was to knock them off the table and kick them around like soccer balls. He had even more fun smashing them and making them into small mountains of "snow." It was useless to try to hide the ornaments in a cabinet or a closet. Okee had already figured out how to open every door and drawer he could reach. He had also learned to climb very well, so there was very little he couldn't reach.

Since the ceiling was about the only safe place, Luke strung a wire from the top frames of two of the kitchen doors. From this wire he hung the little heads. At last they were safe. The wire passed right over Luke's place at the table. From my place I could look up and see the little faces smiling at me while I ate.

Ten days before Christmas, our tree decorations were finished. Not all of the heads survived the beating they took from Okee. Twenty of them were chewed to bits. Five were roasted in the oven because Okee stuffed them in the broiler and we didn't know they were there; six of them Okee hid under the sofa pillows and these were squashed when Luke sat on them; four were drowned in the toilet bowl; eight were stepped on when Okee rolled them under the rug, and ten of them we never did find. Final count showed two hundred finished ones in good condition. I was glad that I had bought extra Styrofoam balls.

Christmas Eve was the time we set up our tree. We were sure this year's tree would not be safe on the floor with a runabout otter. It didn't take us long to decide to tie it to the ceiling, too. Luke was the carpenter, so it was up to him to figure out how to do it. It was a five-foot tree loaded with decorations. I wondered how Luke was going to dangle it from the ceiling without pulling the ceiling down. It took Luke only ten minutes to arrive at a solution.

First, Luke cut the branches from one side of the tree to make it fit in the corner of our living room. Out of some heavy plywood he cut a pie-shaped wedge. This he put on top of the television set, which was three feet off the floor. On top of the wood he placed the tree in its stand. The uppermost branches were tied to the ceiling molding with wire. Now, the tree could not sway one way or the other. All around the bottom of the television Luke put sheets of smooth metal to keep Okee from climbing up on the TV. As an extra precaution he made sure there was no furniture close to the television set that Okee could use as a ladder. With a big smile on his face, Luke backed off and admired his otterproof tree.

Our animals always got toys for Christmas. Most of them were from "Santa Claus." Pierre, my parakeet, always received mirrors or bells for his cage. Trouper got a full-size football every Christmas. This year Trouper got plenty of other toys, too. We wanted to make sure he wouldn't feel jealous because of all the toys that were arriving for Okee.

Okee was well loved by everyone who knew him. Dozens of gifts had come for him by mail or had been personally delivered. By Christmas Eve, Okee's stack of presents took up a whole corner of the room. There was a three-foot-tall plush rabbit dressed in a coat and tie. Two huge beach balls, one orange and one green, were the gifts of Mimi and

The author with Trouper.   ART DOERING

Maryann, Elinor and Marsha, who organized the surprise shower for Okee.

Okee at the age of about six and a half weeks.

Okee loved hamburger.

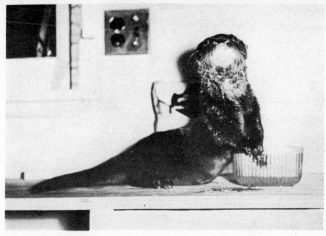

He started to learn about water in a small bowl.

The bathtub became his delight.　　　　　　　　ART DOERING

He liked to put his back foot in his mouth and whirl like a pinwheel.

Investigating the icebox.

Trouper and Okee playing.

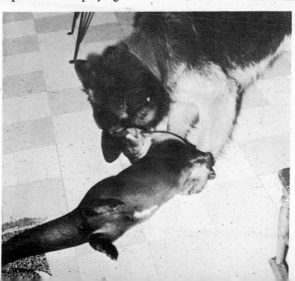

Okee gives the author a loving nip on the ear.   ART DOERING

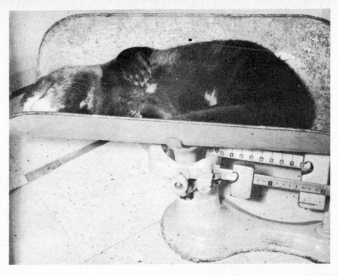

Okee grew at the rate of about one pound and one inch each week.

A quick dip to cool off.

SUNDAY HOME NEWS

Luke, Trouper, and Okee at Stoke's forest.

At home, comfortable in his bed box.

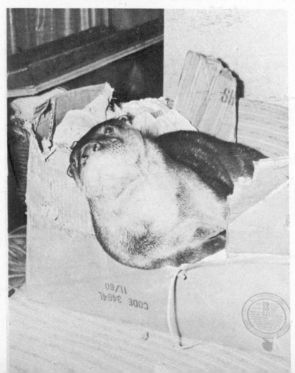

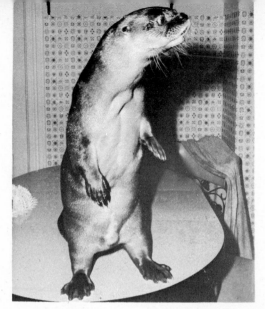

Look at Okee's whiskers and his webbed feet.   ART DOERING

A very serious otter.

Cake on his nose.   ART DOERING

When he had been spanked, the corners of his mouth turned
down.   ART DOERING

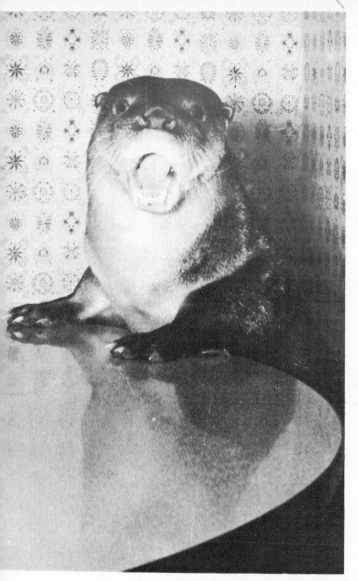

Sometimes he talked a lot.

He could always find a way to get what he wanted. ART DOERING

Playing in the tub.

A place to hide and then peep out.

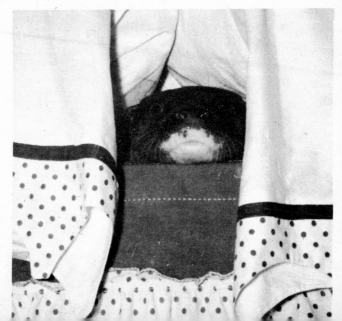

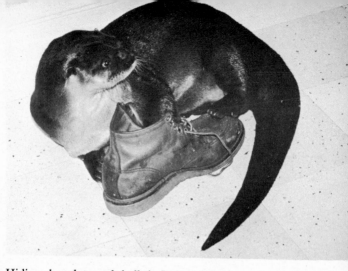

Hiding chocolate malt balls in Luke's shoe.   ART DOERING

Watching the snow fall outside.

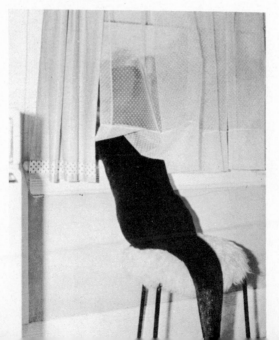

Books never stayed neatly on the shelves.

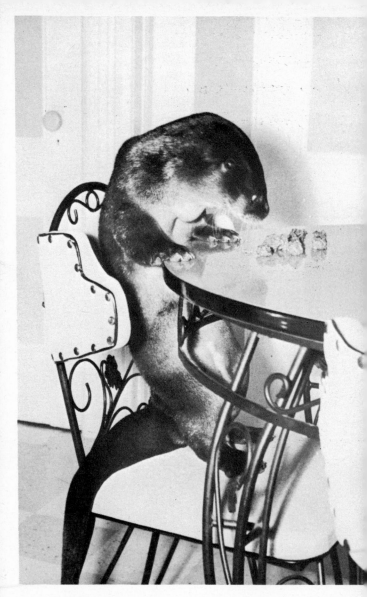

Okee finds a way, as usual.

Joe and Beever at our house.

Beever chewing on Luke's foot.   ART DOERING

"Luke was out of town, and I was left alone with Okee."

ART DOERING

Okee cleaning his paws.   ART DOERING

Okee was a champion swimmer.

Trouper would have liked to get into the tank too.

Underwater games.

His paw is against the glass wall of his tank.   ART DOERING

Elaine, Okee's otter-sitters. Okee's friends from the pet shop gave him a rubber candy cane and a rubber shoe that squeaked. Marsha, the little girl who arranged Okee's baby shower seven months before, came to visit and brought Okee a rubber pork chop. She was very pleased that Okee liked it at once. How he enjoyed tossing it backward over his head! A rubber penguin for his tub was a present from another child at the library.

We had hoped that Trouper would play with his own gifts, but he preferred Okee's. As soon as my back was turned, he would run off with one of Okee's new toys. If I tried to get it back, he would growl at me. Okee didn't mind Trouper stealing his toys. As long as he had his old ping-pong balls, his wooden spool, his bottle caps, and his peach pits, he was perfectly happy. Uusally it was several days, and sometimes several weeks, before he would play with a new toy.

Not all of Okee's gifts were toys. My library assistant gave him a large bath towel which she had made herself. Charlie, our grocer, who supplied Okee's meat, gave him five pounds of hamburger. The man at the tile warehouse gave Okee the biggest gift of all—

eight boxes of ceramic tile. Okee had made many visits to the warehouse with Luke, who bought things there regularly for his work. Once Luke told the man he was going to build a special room in the cellar for Okee. I guess the man thought the only kind of floor an otter couldn't ruin was one made of hard tiles. He was so right!

Okee's best present didn't come until after Christmas. All week long, the weather forecasts had been saying a big snowstorm was coming. I could hardly wait to see what Okee would do in the snow. I had seen pictures of wild otters rolling and jumping and sliding down snowy hills. I wondered if Okee would enjoy snow as much as his wild relatives did.

We had been getting Okee ready for snow and cold weather ever since early autumn. Each day we kept him out for longer periods of time. By Christmas he was so used to the cold weather that he could stay outside for as long as two hours without catching a cold. Of course, wild otters are outside all the time. Since they don't hibernate like woodchucks and bears, they must search for food all winter. I have read that in very cold places like Wisconsin or Minnesota, otters must search for fish in water that is thick with ice. We were not thinking of dunking Okee in an ice-cold river. Living in a warm house had made him too delicate for that. Perhaps in another year we would try it. First we had to see how he would do in deep snow.

The snowfall we had been waiting for began in the early evening four days after Christmas. It was a steady fall with large soft flakes that piled up inches of snow very rapidly. It was perfect weather for a long hike. I felt sure that the thick layer of fat under Okee's skin and his double coat of fur would keep him warm while we were walking. I worried, though, about the biting wind that started to blow. To be sure Okee didn't get chilled in case we should stop along the way, I dressed him in a dog coat. I should say jacket, for Okee was much longer than the average dog. He looked so funny—like a man wearing a shirt and no pants. Perhaps the next time I bought him a coat I should try one made for a dachshund.

It had been snowing for two hours when we started out. Luke and Trouper trudged along in the lead, and Okee and I followed. The snow was up to Okee's chin in most places, and over his head in others. Even with his short legs, he seemed to have no trouble keeping up with Luke and Trouper. He soon learned he could get through the snow even faster if he tunneled underneath it. It was a strange feeling, walking along holding a leash that moved but seemed to have nothing attached to it. Okee would be walking along on top of the snow when all of a sudden he would dive underneath it. Without moving the snow on top at all, he would push himself along on his chest. His front feet he kept tucked at his sides, but he used his hind feet to propel himself. When he had traveled this way eight or ten feet, he would pop his head up out of the snow and look back at me with a silly grin on his face. He seemed to be saying, "Here I am!" or, "Ha! Ha! You can't catch me."

There was no doubt about it. Okee loved the snow as much as any small child. He could run and slide, roll and tumble, run and slide so fast I could hardly keep up with him.

As I watched, I could not help admiring this happy-go-lucky clown. He was the merriest, best-natured animal I had ever known.

10

*O*kee had lived with us less than a year, but Luke and I were already beginning to show signs of exhaustion. I had circles under my eyes down to my chin from lack of sleep. Luke walked around evenings bent over like an old man from being so tired. But Okee hadn't slowed down one bit. Like his wild relatives, the weasels and the minks, Okee was on the move every minute he was awake. The weasel family of animals is known for its endless energy, and Okee was doing his best to act like a typical weasel. It takes much patience and endurance to live with an animal that hardly ever sits still. Perhaps the average person would have given up and shipped Okee off to a zoo. But we both loved Okee dearly and would never part with him.

We had learned months before that an otter isn't really happy unless he is busy. To keep himself busy, Okee created mischief. Of course, he didn't know it was mischief. He was just having fun in his own little otter way. At least a dozen times a day I caught him rocking the stand of Pierre's cage. He seemed to be trying to shake the bird from his perch.

When he wasn't after the bird, he was rolling the apples and oranges out of the fruit bowl and down the cellar steps. If he thought no one was looking, he would run about the house picking up all the small things he could find. Pieces of candy and bottle caps he hid in the wastepaper baskets. Shoes and paper cups were stuffed in the garbage can. After everything was safely hidden, he would gallop through the house and knock over all the containers. Then he would search among the trash for his hidden treasures. By the time he found them all, my rooms looked like the beach at low tide.

At a time when most people are in bed, I would still be up, trying to put my house back in order. I sometimes wondered why I bothered. The next night would find everything undone again. Rugs no longer lay flat on my floors. They were always rippled like washboards from being crumpled by a playful otter sliding on them. Shirts and socks hung out of half-opened bureau drawers, left that way by an otter who was trying to hide his toys under the clothes.

I often wondered why I ever made beds in the morning. Okee had his own ideas how a bed should be made. To an otter, a bed isn't comfortable unless it has mountains of twisted, tangled covers. He could get into a bed, burrow under the covers, and in no time at all have the blankets and sheets erupting like little volcanoes. By doing corkscrew rolls with the corner of a sheet in his mouth, he could tie the sheet into knots. Not one bit of bedding was missed. Sheets were pulled over blankets; blankets were pulled over bedspreads. Then Okee would slide down the spread, skid across the room on a rug, and run off to make mischief somewhere else.

Books never remained neatly lined up on my shelves. Okee would get behind the books and push them all off. Then he could hide things in the pages. I didn't always find his little "treasures" right away. Days later, I would pick up a dictionary or a prayer book and find their pages marked with potato peelings or wads of gum which Okee had stolen from the garbage can.

I remember a cold night, a few months after Christmas, when Luke went into the closet to get a pair of shoes he had not worn for a long time. They had been next to a heating pipe since the beginning of winter. As Luke put on the right shoe, he remarked how warm it was. As he put on the left one, I heard him moan. Slowly he took his foot out of the shoe. There, clinging to the toe of his white sock, was a soggy chocolate-covered malt ball, one of many Christmas goodies Okee had stolen and hidden away. It was partly melted after weeks of being in the toe of a warm shoe.

I have always felt that most of the time Okee really didn't mean to break things. But even though I could usually understand why Okee's "accidents" happened, the damage was just as great as if he had set out to destroy things on purpose. Take, for instance, his habit of swinging on the hanging vines I kept over the bedroom window. I had only myself to blame for that. When Okee was a baby, I taught him to jump at things I dangled in front of him, like a ball on a string or a balloon on a stick. How could I blame him then for swinging from the vines that hung so low he could reach them by standing on the tops of the bureaus? How was he to know the difference between a string and a vine when both made just as much fun?

I guess I should have been understanding, too, when Okee ruined the decoration on one whole wall in our bedroom. Luke and I had spent much time and money pasting expensive, bright-red cloth instead of wallpaper on one wall of our bedroom. One night, when we were busy in another part of the house, Okee unraveled all the edges of the strips of cloth we had just put up, trying to get to the wheat paste underneath. Okee was as fond of wheat paste as a cat is of catnip. Smelling and licking paste made him act as if he were drunk. Knowing why he did it didn't make me feel any better about my once beautiful wall. Maybe he didn't deserve it, but Okee got a sound spanking.

When Okee was in a room, I could not sit quietly behind a newspaper and read it. Okee loved to leap into the air and dive through a newspaper, like a circus dog jumping through a hoop. Once I was sitting in the living-room chair looking at a picture of the President in the newspaper. All of a sudden, the picture exploded, and in its place was an otter's face, followed, of course, by otter feet and tail. I couldn't scold Okee, for I had taught him to jump at a towel when I held it up. To Okee, I guess a newspaper held up looked very much like a towel.

Okee always took the shortest distance to get wherever he wanted to go. He couldn't be bothered going around something. It was much quicker to go through it or over it. That's how my floor lamps got broken. Okee liked to hide behind the sofa and pounce on people that went by. It so happened there was a floor lamp on either end of the sofa. If he took time to run around the lamps, the person he was waiting for might get past the sofa safely. So, when the victim approached one end of the sofa, Okee would dive through the legs of the lamp on the opposite end of the sofa and pounce. This game was hard on the lamps, and even harder on the shades. We now keep on hand at all times a large roll of plastic. When the shades become riddled with holes, we simply cut off a piece of plastic and make new ones. It is amazing how clever we have become since Okee came to live with us!

Sometimes, though, I think Okee is cleverer still. To keep him in either the kitchen or the living room, I would often close the half door between the two rooms. The door was four feet high, too high for an ordinary otter to get over, but not for Okee. Three feet away from the door in the living room was a chair. All Okee had to do was climb up on the back of the chair and jump over the door into the kitchen from there.

I thought I would outsmart Okee by moving the chair eight feet away. I had seen Okee jump off the back of the sofa and land as much as five feet away, but never farther.

was sure I had him fooled this time. But I was wrong. Okee knew he couldn't jump the eight feet from the chair to the door, so he just waited for something he could use as a step. That something turned out to be Trouper.

When Trouper happened to walk over to the door and stand there, Okee knew at once what to do. He jumped up on the back of the chair, leaped out into space, and landed on the dog's back. In a move as fast as lightning, he came down with his hind feet, up with his front feet, and caught the edge of the door. In an instant he was over it. It happened so fast Okee was on the kitchen floor on the other side of the door when Trouper fell to the living-room floor from the push on his back.

As the months went by, I found I was making more and more changes in my house for Okee. An active, growing otter had to have room to play. Pieces of furniture that weren't necessary I gave away. I kept only the sturdiest tables and chairs. Fragile table lamps were stored away in the attic to wait for the time when Okee grew up and no longer destroyed things. Little did I know that time would never come. Breakable knickknacks were put up on high shelves. Some of my rooms looked as if I were getting them ready for a flood.

Fancy bureau scarves and doilies were removed from all the furniture. Okee liked to play magician and try to yank the doily out from under the ashtray without upsetting the tray. I saw him do the trick right only once. Every other time, the ashtrays would tumble to the floor, spilling ashes and cigarette butts all over my rug.

I had become a better-than-average housekeeper, thanks to Okee. I found it was better to put my things neatly away than to have to keep picking them up once Okee found them. With Okee about, I could no longer leave dishes and leftover food on the table after a meal. Unless I took everything off right away, Okee would clear the table for me. If I was careless and left a container of milk on the table, I could be sure I wouldn't find it standing upright when I returned. Okee liked milk, but since he couldn't lap it from a dish like a cat, I didn't give it to him in liquid form. Instead, I put powdered milk in his hamburger formula. It didn't matter to Okee that he couldn't lap. Whenever he spotted a container of milk on the table, he would climb up and knock it over. Then he would lie on the floor underneath the table and catch the stream of milk as it spilled over the edge. If Okee wanted something badly enough, he could figure a way to get it.

Since Okee was a very curious animal, closed doors, cabinets, or drawers were an invitation to him to find out what was on the other side. I remember how easily he learned to open the kitchen cabinets. Okee had an amazing memory and was able to imitate things he had seen us do days or even weeks earlier. I had a feeling I should not have let Okee see how I fastened the lower cabinets. How serious he looked as he watched me slide a ruler through the handles to keep the cabinet doors shut. Somehow I felt he was remembering this. I really wasn't too surprised a few days later when I found he had removed the ruler that was supposed to keep him out of the cabinets. He not only removed the ruler, he also discovered how many wonderful boxes there were inside, just waiting to be emptied. From then on, all Okee needed was a few minutes and he would have the kitchen floor covered with piles of corn flakes, heaps of flour, and hills of dried beans. Okee used to pull the sugar bowl out of the cabinet and dump it almost every day, until I moved it to a higher place. Sugar made wonderful play water when he couldn't get the wet kind. He just loved to swim through the sugar across the kitchen floor.

After we had moved Okee's home to the basement, we had tried putting slide bolts or turn catches on the cabinets there. But that hadn't discouraged Okee from ransacking them. In fact, a locked cabinet was a challenge to be met and overcome. Simple locks he pulled apart or picked open with his toenails. Heavy padlocks he couldn't open, but that didn't stop him from getting into a cabinet. Using all his super-strength, he simply pulled on the lower corner of the cabinet door with his two front paws. When he pulled the door out far enough to get his head in, it was no problem squeezing the rest of his body through the opening. When he wanted to get out, he pushed with his head and shoulders as hard as he could against the same corner of the door he pulled to get in. He could then crawl out again, usually dragging some forbidden object with him.

Eventually Luke found one lock that Okee couldn't open. Although Okee learned to unscrew jar lids with his front paws, he could not use his paws well enough to open snap buckles. Thumbs are needed to open these, and Okee had no thumbs. With snap buckles on both the tops and bottoms of all the wooden doors, Okee could not pry them open. In case he thought about prying to pull the doors apart in the middle, Luke fastened the centers with slide bolts and turn catches. Every wooden cabinet door in the basement was now fastened in four places. The doors and drawers of all the metal cabinets were fastened with metal screws. Unless Okee learns to use a screwdriver, he cannot open these. But Okee does not give up easily. Some day I knew he will find another way to get into the cabinets.

Life with Okee was never dull. When he outgrew one kind of mischief, he replaced it with another kind. For a while it was the wall telephone that interested him the most. He would climb up on the stool near the phone and remove the receiver from the hook. While it was dangling in space, he would put a little webbed claw into one of the holes on the disk and spin the dial. I'm not sure whether it was the holes or the sound the dial made as it was spinning that fascinated him the most. Thank heavens his combinations of numbers never caused anyone's phone to ring.

Okee's interest in the telephone lasted for several months. One morning we awoke to find that Okee had chewed the telephone cord into twelve little pieces. The rest of the phone looked as if it had been chewed by a bear. I should have paid a large sum to have the telephone replaced, but the repairman was very kind. He said no one in his office would believe him if he told them the telephone had been eaten by an otter. So he simply said in his report that our white phone had discolored. He gave us a new one free.

11

I had been thinking for some time that Okee
and Beever should meet. Okee had yet to
discover there were other otters in the world.
I didn't want to buy another otter, but I
thought it would be nice if Okee could have a
playmate once in a while. With this in mind,
we packed Okee and Trouper in the car and
made our second trip to Joe's house.

Beever behaved nicely this time, so Joe
agreed to let the two otters meet. Okee and
Beever scolded and screamed to each other,
but neither one tried to bite the other. Beever did swat at Okee, but Okee was polite and

did not try to hit back. Instead, he put his paws in front of his face to keep from getting hit in the eye by Beever's wild punches. Since Okee was still much bigger and stronger than Beever, I was glad there was no fight.

Before we left that night, Joe said he was thinking of taking a trip to the Maryland Zoo. He had a problem, though. He couldn't find anyone to care for Beever while he was gone. I don't know why I did it. Our house was too small for even one otter. We hardly had enough patience for our own little demon. But I volunteered. And that's how we ended up taking Beever to Atlantic City.

Joe had promised to call me a week before his trip. Weeks went by and there was no phone call. Then one Sunday afternoon there was Joe's voice on the phone, very timid, saying, "I'm leaving for Maryland Tuesday. Is that too soon?"

Oh, horrors! I thought. Tuesday! It was already Sunday. On Wednesday, Luke and I were leaving for a library convention at Atlantic City. We had already decided to take the dog, the bird, and the otter with us. While I went to meetings at Atlantic City, Luke would stay with the animals at a friend's home ten miles away. It was a large summer home, and our friend did not mind if it got a little soiled or wet. If we agreed to care for Beever as we promised, we would have to take him along too. But a promise is a promise. I could not say no now.

Joe warned me that Beever was not used to traveling. He said Beever would probably make a big fuss in the car. I assured him we could manage, and it was all set.

Joe and Beever arrived at our house on Monday night so Joe could stay with Beever overnight before leaving for Maryland. Having Joe there with him made Beever feel right at home. He found a place behind the living-room sofa where he could "ha" at whoever came near him. After a while, he stopped "ha'ing." When I looked behind the sofa, I found him chewing merrily away at the sponge-rubber pad under my rug. The edge of the pad had been straight. When Beever finished with it, it looked as if someone had made designs in it with a jigsaw.

At bedtime, Beever roamed restlessly about the house for a while. He poked around in all the corners, then ended up chirping and pulling on Joe's blankets. Joe lifted him into the bed, and the house quieted down enough for everyone to sleep.

Next morning I fed Okee his breakfast, then locked him in the cellar while I tried to feed Beever. For some reason I could not understand, Beever was back to hating me again. Whenever I came near him, he would growl. I decided to wait for Joe to get up and let him feed Beever. But I couldn't help wondering what I was going to do if Beever refused to eat after Joe left.

Beever's growls might have frightened me, but they didn't frighten Luke. He walked up to Beever and picked him up before Beever realized what was happening. Beever was so surprised he forgot to growl. Luke talked to him firmly but stroked him gently. In a few minutes he had won Beever over. It was no problem then for Luke to coax Beever to eat. Once I learned to risk being bitten, and show Beever who was boss, I too could make him behave.

The rest of the morning Joe and I spent watching the otters while they played outdoors. We knew we could not keep our eyes on two otters at the same time, so we let them out one at a time. Beever was first, but he didn't give us any trouble. He was timid about going too far away from Joe. Beever really loved Joe and expected Joe to protect him.

The next hour belonged to Okee, and he made the most of it. Joe soon realized how tiring it was to keep up with him. Okee led us on a merry chase—over the fence to Trouper's pen, under the gate, into the garage, through the flower beds into the garden, and around the house. If Beever ever learned to climb and jump like Okee, how would Joe ever manage him alone?

By 4 P.M. Tuesday, Joe was on his way. The rest of the afternoon and evening Luke and I spent feeding, walking, bathing, and amusing two lively otters. By midnight we had given Okee ten baths and Beever five. Hardly was one otter out of the tub and dried than the other was ready to go in. Every chair, windowsill, and doorknob in the house was draped with a wet towel or rug. Everything was so damp it seemed almost as if it was raining inside.

The next morning we made the mistake of turning both otters loose in the house at the same time. Poor Trouper! As number-three otter-sitter in our family, he had learned to take as many abuses from Okee as we did. Trouper could not walk across the floor without having Okee hanging on to his feet. He would pick his feet up high to shake Okee off. After a while he developed a strut like a drum majorette leading a parade. But now, with both Beever and Okee to worry about, he didn't know which way to go. He was used to chasing Okee out of places he shouldn't be in, but minding two otters had him all mixed up.

First, Okee got in the dish closet and he had to pull him out. As soon as Okee was out, Beever got in, so Trouper had to pull him out. While Trouper was trying to keep Okee off the kitchen table, Beever was climbing all over the chairs. If Okee wasn't snapping open the oven door, Beever was snapping open the broiler door. While Okee was upsetting the garbage can, Beever was upsetting the wastepaper basket. All this was too much for Trouper. He just couldn't be everywhere at once. Finally, when he could think of nothing else to do, he sat in the middle of the kitchen floor and howled. We had to admit that two otters and a dog were two too many. Trouper was put outside in his pen. From then on, only one otter at a time was let loose.

It took all day and part of the night for me to pack for our trip. Not until 11 P.M. had I finished packing all the things I thought we might need for us and the animals. There seemed to be enough baggage for a family of five about to go on a six-week camping trip. It took another hour for Luke to jam everything into the back of the station wagon.

Each otter was put in his own cage. Luke placed the two cages, side by side, on the floor behind the front seats, where I could watch them easily. Because the cages were so wide, they were a few inches apart. To avoid any trouble between the otters, Luke draped blankets over the sides of the cages that faced each other. If they couldn't see each other, they wouldn't scream at one another. At least that's what we thought. After the baggage and the otters were put in the car, there was only a small space near the rear door left for Trouper. It was good he didn't mind being cramped. The last to go in the car was Pierre, the parakeet, who had his own little traveling cage.

I had planned this trip very carefully, but still I had a feeling something was going to go wrong. I did not have long to wait. We had traveled only one block when Okee stuck his paw out of his cage. Feeling around for something he could play with, he accidentally poked his paw into Beever's cage. It so happened Beever's nose was in the way. Beever didn't like being poked in the nose, so he let out a terrible scream. Okee was so surprised he did something he had done only once or twice before in his life. He fired his little musk gun.

That odor was bad enough in a large room. In an automobile with the windows shut, it was dreadful. However, it was well after midnight and we had a long trip ahead. We had started out so late we didn't want to stop only a block from home to let the car air out. And yet, if we rode along with the windows open, the bird or the otters might catch a cold. There was nothing to do but grin and bear it for the next twenty minutes until the odor went away. And that's what we did.

For the rest of the trip, Okee thought it

was great fun to poke his paws into Beever's cage and make him yell. Beever did his best to avoid trouble, but Okee kept teasing. After ten minutes of it, Beever's patience wore out. From then on, whenever Okee tried to put his paws into Beever's cage, Beever would reach out and slap Okee. Then Okee would scream. What started out as play turned out to be a real honest-to-goodness otter boxing bout.

It was 3:30 in the morning when we arrived at Atlantic City. Luke and I wanted to go to bed right away, but Beever and Okee saw to it that we couldn't. They had stored up plenty of energy during the three and a half hours they were in their cages. Now they were anxious to eat, swim, and play. I had lived with an otter long enough to know that he is not very patient. He never gives up until he has his own way.

So, at a time when most people are sound asleep, we were up watching otters swim in the bathroom.

The next two days were hectic but fun. We proved to our own satisfaction that we could manage two otters very well. Both Okee and Beever were as good as we could expect any otter to be. When Joe arrived on Friday to take Beever home, we went for one last walk along the beach. Then, in another hour, we were packed and on our way home.

I told Joe, as we said goodbye, that if he ever wanted to leave Beever with us again, it would be no trouble at all for us to take care of him. Little did I know then just how much trouble there was going to be.

12

*I*t was the first week in June. Luke was out of town working, and I was left alone with Okee. Until now, there were two of us to share the work. But five days alone with Okee were almost more than I could manage. Somehow, I had more problems with Okee in those five days than Luke and I had together in a month.

Okee always walked nicely for Luke, but when I took him for his evening romp he would wiggle out of his harness. Then he would lead me on a merry chase, across lawns, through people's back yards, and over their porches. I usually had to chase him for two blocks before I caught him. Then I would have to steer him all the way home by holding on to his tail. There were many times I was thankful for that long heavy tail.

One day in the bath he almost scalded himself by turning on the hot water full force. But that was nothing compared to the day he decided to explore the sewer.

The storm sewer by the corner of our yard fascinated Okee. Whenever he was allowed to run free, he always headed there. More than once, Luke or I had to make a flying tackle to catch him before he vanished into the pipe.

On this day, Okee was playing in his plastic pool in the center of the yard. I turned my back for a few minutes to plant some flowers. When I looked again, Okee was not in his pool. At first I thought he might have wandered out into the road. Okee was not afraid of cars. Like a small child, he never bothered to look one way or the other when he darted across the street after something. I ran to the corner and called, but Okee was nowhere in sight.

For five minutes I called him, but still no Okee. Wherever he was, he must have heard me, but he was very stubborn. He only came when he wanted to. As I stood there wondering what to do next, someone called from the park across the street.

"Hey, lady!" I looked up and saw a young boy waving in my direction. "Are you looking for that thing with a long tail that looks like a muskrat?" he asked.

"Yes," I said. I didn't bother to tell him that otters are not at all like muskrats. "Did you see him?" I asked anxiously.

"Yes," the boy answered. "He just went down the sewer." For a moment I was overcome by panic. The sewer pipe emptied into the main line under the middle of the road. The main line ended at the canal only two blocks away. If Okee got into the main pipe and followed it to the canal, I might never find him. Okee liked to explore strange places. I knew he wouldn't come back until he was ready. He might even lose his way. I got down on my hands and knees and peered down into the catch basin. Frantically I called, "Okee! Okee!" hoping he would hear my voice and follow it. There was no sound but the echo of my own voice.

By this time, some of the young boy's

friends had gathered at the corner to help me. If they could get the cover off the catch basin, one of them could go down into the pipe to look for Okee. They tried and tried to lift it, but the cover would not budge. We stood there helplessly.

Suddenly our ears caught a faint sloshing noise. At first it was far away, but as we listened, it came closer. It sounded like a child in rubber boots splashing through mud puddles. Quickly we all got down on our hands and knees and peered into the sewer. "Slosh, slosh, slosh, slosh," came the sound, closer and closer. Then out of the murky darkness appeared an otter. He was covered with black mud and dripping from eyes, ears, nose, chin, and every last whisker.

"Grab him!" I shouted to the closest boy. Before he could get his arm down the hole, Okee had disappeared underneath the road. While we were looking down one catch basin, Okee crossed over to the catch basin on the other side of the road. He paid no attention to our calls. Back and forth, back and forth he went, careful to keep out of reach of the arms waiting to grab him.

It was foolish to hope that Okee would

come out on his own. He was having too much fun playing hide-and-go-seek. If only I could find a child small enough to crawl down into the catch basin, he might be able to grab Okee when he came through the pipe. There were several small boys standing nearby. I asked two of them, but they were afraid to try. Then a little red-haired boy about eight years old pushed his way through the crowd.

"I'll do it," he said, and with that he crawled down into the sewer. He landed at the edge of the pipe at the same time Okee was coming through. The otter was so surprised to find someone there that he stopped for a moment. That was all the time the boy needed to grab him and pass him up to me. He was covered with sticky mud, but that didn't matter. I was so happy to see him I gave him a big hug.

I'm sure the little boy never knew how grateful I felt. I watched him ride away on his bicycle. He was beaming with joy over the dollar I had given him as a reward. In my heart I was glad for one little boy who took time to be kind.

Joe had told me many times that some day I would learn how hard it was to care for an otter all alone. I had often teased him about his problems with Beever. Now it was his turn to laugh at me. I wrote him a long letter about Okee's latest adventures.

Joe's answer to my letter came very quickly. As I expected, he teased me a bit. "Why don't you sue the city for having a sewer that an otter can crawl into?" he wrote. "Then take the money you get and buy a fence to keep Okee in the yard." Maybe the fence wouldn't be such a bad idea, I thought. But with Okee's climbing skill, it would have to be at least twenty-five feet high to keep him in the yard.

Joe ended his letter by telling me he was going to California soon on zoo business. Did we really want to have Beever as a house guest again? Of course we did, I wrote back.

A few weeks later, on a Sunday, Joe arrived at our house with Beever, his traveling cage, his towels, and his toys. While we ate dinner, Beever roamed about our house, sniffing at everything he remembered from his last visit. It wasn't long before he settled down in his favorite spot behind the sofa and went to sleep.

After dinner, Okee was let up out of the basement to greet his furry guest. Okee was anything but gentle with Beever this time. But Beever soon proved he was not the least bit afraid of Okee, even though Okee weighed almost twice as much as he did. When he had enough rough play, he bit Okee on the foot and nose. It happened so quickly Okee had no chance to move away. The bite was not bad, but it taught Okee to respect this pint-sized otter who showed no fear.

Later on that hot Sunday afternoon, we packed the otters in our car and took a ride to a mountain stream three miles away. The stream was clear and cold. It was far enough back in the mountains to be perfectly clean. This was important to the health of our otters. They had spent most of their lives indoors, so outside germs would be new to them. The fewer new germs they met, the less chance there would be for them to become ill. Since many trout lived in the stream, I felt sure the water would be safe for our otters. We attached a twelve-foot-long lead to each otter's harness and in they went.

How they enjoyed that water! For three hours we watched as they played, sometimes alone and sometimes together. They looked like porpoises leaping through the ocean waves as they shot up out of the water in a fast game of tag. Sometimes they arched their backs and necks and wriggled up to the surface and then down again, just like eels. When they tired of playing together, they invented their own games to play by themselves. Beever, who was the faster swimmer, made practice dives from a large rock. Okee had more fun skimming along the bottom of the stream in search of underwater treasures. Here at last they were performing as nature had meant them to. How beautiful they looked!

I had thought that the fact that they had been hand fed for months would have destroyed whatever instincts the otters had for catching their own food. I was wrong. They chased or played with whatever water creatures they could find, just as their wild relatives would have done. Okee even ate a small fish he caught, but Beever chose to play with the tadpole he captured.

It pleased Joe to see his otter so happy with his new friends. Now he could leave his pet and go away with no worries.

Beever felt at home in our house almost at once. He played with the dog and went walking with Luke just as Okee did. Luke and Beever became such good friends that Luke almost forgot about Okee. Okee didn't seem to mind as long as he had plenty to eat and plenty of water for swimming. I was pleased to see that Beever was eating so well. Often an animal will refuse to eat when he is taken to a strange place. At home, Beever ate only three meals a day, but at our house he was eating six. No doubt he needed the extra food because he was so much more active.

Our happiness did not last long. Joe had been gone only a few days when Beever took sick. His illness came without warning. One day he was fine, and the next day he felt so bad he refused to eat. He was listless and his eyes looked dull and glassy. He didn't want to play or swim. All he wanted to do was sleep. Sleep often helps more than medicine, so I let him sleep for a long while. When he awoke, Luke offered him food, but again he refused it. Joe had told us Beever was very fond of cottage cheese, so we tried to coax him to eat some. He refused that, too.

The next day, Beever was much worse. Just the sight of food made him gag. Some animals can last for days without eating, but not otters. There was no time to waste. We had to get him to a veterinarian at once. After examining Beever, the doctor thought he had an infection in his intestines. The infection seemed to be like the one Beever had had the April before. The doctor decided to give him a shot of the same medicine that had cured him the last time. To make sure all the germs were killed, the doctor gave us some more medicine to give Beever at home.

By evening, Beever was a little better. He ate some cottage cheese. Then we fed him some Esbilac (milk). After his meal, he went to sleep and slept soundly till morning. I knew it took only a day or two for otters to get sick enough to die. I also knew they could get better just as quickly if medicine was given in time. Somehow I felt that Beever would be well in a few days.

The next day, Beever was worse again. He wouldn't eat anything at all and even water made him vomit. Still, I tried not to worry. Perhaps a second shot would help. So, off to the vet's we went, with Beever crying in great distress. Nothing we did seemed to comfort him.

For three days, Luke and I took turns watching Beever day and night. Each night we prayed he would get better. I thought about Joe somewhere out West enjoying his trip and thinking that all was well with his pet. Somehow I would have to reach him and tell him Beever was very, very sick. If only he could fly back to New Jersey and be with Beever, it might give Beever the will to live. It was just a small chance, but it was worth a try.

I did not know where Joe was, but I was sure the zoo did. Two hours after I phoned Joe's secretary, I received a call from Joe. He was in New Mexico, but he said he would try to get a plane back to New Jersey.

Joe called several times that day. Each time it broke my heart to have to tell him that Beever was worse. First he had chills, and we wrapped him in blankets to keep him warm. Then he ran a high fever and we had to put cold cloths on his head to make him cool. All night long, we did this. Oh, how I wished Joe could be with his pet, but there was no plane to New Jersey until the next day. For Beever, there was no next day. He died that morning.

In the short time that he was with us, we had learned to love Beever. Though he pretended to be fierce, he was really gentle. He was quiet compared to Okee, but in many ways he was so much more lovable. Luke missed his little friend so much he could not hold back the tears. I cried too, not only for Beever, but for Joe and the loneliness he would soon have to face.

13

We were so upset over Beever's illness and death that we did not realize Okee was becoming ill. I noticed he was sleeping more than usual and eating less, but I didn't worry about him. Perhaps he was feeling hurt, I thought, because we had not paid much attention to him. He was sneezing and coughing quite a bit, but he had done that since he was a baby. I had made up my mind a long time before that he was allergic to house dust. His eyes and nose were running too, but our vet seemed to feel that was natural for otters out of water. There was one symptom that disturbed me, though. He was having great difficulty swallowing. He acted as if he had a very sore throat.

Two days after Beever's death, Okee became extremely listless. He moped about the house, refusing to play or swim. I was sure now that there was something wrong. But he roused himself for his evening romp with Trouper, and I decided not to call the vet that night. Okee played so hard and so rough that I was sure he could not be sick. I was wrong.

When Okee did not get up for breakfast the next day, I went to wake him. I thought it was strange that he would not open his eyes, even when I held a piece of fresh meat under his nose. He didn't want to eat, so I had to force the meat down his throat. Every other piece made him gag, and he kept grabbing at his throat with his paws.

At supper he did the same thing. Instead of going to sleep as he usually did after a meal, he raced frantically about the house. He acted as if he did not know where he was going or what he was doing. Every few minutes he went looking for a drink. Otters do drink plenty of water, but never before had I seen him drink that much. Between drinks, he rolled and thrashed about on the floor as if he were in great pain. Then he started to cry in the same pitiful way Beever had cried just before he died. There was no doubt in my mind that Okee had the same disease that had killed Beever.

By 11 P.M. that evening, Okee was in the animal hospital. His appointment was with Dr. North, one of the finest veterinarians in the country. For twenty years I had known this kind, gentle man who loved all his animal patients. Dr. North knew a great deal about many animals. He did not believe in destroying an animal if there was even the slightest chance he might get well. I knew Dr. North had never treated an otter before, but I was sure if anyone could save Okee's life, he could.

So little is known about otters that Dr. North did not want to risk giving Okee too strong a medicine. Both Beever and Okee had all the symptoms of a serious disease called cat distemper. The disease almost always kills the animal that comes down with it. No one knew for sure if otters could get distemper. Zoo veterinarians knew that many baby otters died suddenly, but they did not always know what had killed them. If Dr. North injected Okee with cat serum, the medicine might help him. But, if Okee was allergic to the serum, it could kill him. Dr. North did not want to take that chance unless Okee got much worse. He decided to try a milder but safer medicine first.

Okee was given an injection that Thursday night in the hospital, and another the following night. At home we gave him more medicine. We mixed it with milk and squirted it into his mouth with a syringe. He was very good about taking his medicine, but we had to force him to eat. The medicine helped him a little at first. For a while he could breathe better and he even felt like playing. Dr. North was so pleased with Okee's improvement he decided not to give him another injection on Saturday. It would be better, he said, to let Okee's body rest for a day.

We all expected Okee to feel better by Sunday morning, but he didn't. He was much worse. He could barely open his eyes, and he was so weak he could hardly walk. The inside of his mouth, which once was a healthy red, was now almost white. His coat was no longer beautiful and glossy. Instead, it was rough and dull. Dry sneezes had become wet sneezes. It was so hard for him to swallow that he wouldn't eat any food at all. We couldn't even force the food down his throat. By 9 P.M. that evening, Okee was so sick I didn't think he would live until his ten o'clock appointment at the vet's.

When we arrived at the hospital, the doctor was waiting for Okee. He had the medicine all ready to give him at once. Quickly Okee was placed in a small cage so he could not bite while he was being given the needles. No one knew any better than Luke how hard even a very sick otter can bite when he is in pain. In the past week Luke had been badly bitten three times, twice by Beever and once by Okee. Luke did not want to take any chances this time trying to hold Okee with his hands. Instead, he pulled Okee's tail through the bars of the cage. Then, while he hung on as tightly as he could, the doctor injected three needles into the muscle of Okee's tail. The needles hurt so that Okee screamed and grabbed the blanket in his cage. In just a few seconds, he had ripped it to ribbons.

All the next day Okee grew worse. He did not even pick his head up when we spoke to him. He just lay on the floor in the bathroom as if he didn't even know we were there. Was this going to be the last day we would see Okee alive?

Okee's heartbeat and his breathing had been slowing down all afternoon. In another two hours he lay near death. I tried not to think about it. He was so young—only a little over a year old. Just last week he had been so playful and happy. I would give anything now to see him turning my house topsy-turvy again. "Okee, you can't die," I kept saying, but he was dying and I could do nothing to stop it.

Okee's fourth appointment at the vet's was for 11 P.M. It was several hours past the doctor's regular visiting hours, but he made a special trip to his office to see Okee. I did not think Dr. North could save his life now, but Luke said we must not give up. Okee was limp and almost lifeless when Luke carried him into the doctor's office. His once plump body was no more than skin and bones.

Dr. North took one look at Okee and said there was only one chance left to save his life.

If we would give our permission, he would inject Okee with the cat serum at once. The serum might help him, or, Dr. North warned us, it might kill him. Without the serum, he would die anyhow. If this was Okee's last chance at life, we had to give it to him. And so the serum was given, along with other medicines to make it work faster. All we could do now was to wait and pray.

Dr. North told us the medicine might make Okee do strange things. We didn't expect it to act so quickly, though. Ten minutes after we arrived home, Okee was running around the house madly. For an hour he jumped at the doors, at the windows, and on the counters. We were afraid that he would soon drop dead if we did not do something to stop him. There was nothing we could do but catch him and lock him in his cage. We hoped this would quiet him, but it didn't.

It took Okee only a few seconds to push apart the bars of his cage and crawl through. Round and round the house he ran, biting and snapping at anything in his path. Mad as he was, he never once tried to bite Luke or me. Then, just as suddenly as it began, the madness left him. He dropped to the floor and crawled on his belly into the bathroom. I had made a bed of soft blankets in the darkest corner, but he pulled the bedding out. As I watched, he rolled over on his back on the cold floor. Then he gave a big yawn and in less than a minute he fell into a deep sleep.

By morning, Okee felt much better. He could walk and run, and he even felt well enough to clean his toenails. Every night for a week Okee went to the doctor for an injection of serum. He screamed and cried and ripped his blanket to shreds at every needle. When it was over, he seemed to forgive us at once for the pain we made him bear. I think he knew we were trying to make him better.

For thirty-three days Luke and I kept watch over Okee. We took turns sleeping and eating so one of us would always be with him. We squirted medicine down his throat six times a day and force-fed him some soft food every three hours. We fed him a spoonful of water every half hour and wrapped his head in cold wet towels whenever he became hot. Eight times a day, one of us carried him to his litter pan in the basement and then carried him upstairs again. Dr. North said

Okee must not climb stairs, for he needed to save his energy.

To make sure Okee stayed warm and dry while he was so very sick, we let him sleep in our bed. Caring for such a sick animal took a great deal of time, patience, and energy. Luke and I were very, very tired, but we would not give up. Okee's life depended on our care.

The medicine Dr. North was giving Okee made him feel quite peppy. It also gave him a very large and unusual appetite. For eight days we had tried to coax Okee to eat. Now that he was eating, we had to try even harder to make him stop. The doctor told us to give him only a little bit of food at a time. Too much all at once could kill him, he said, but we couldn't make Okee understand that.

Besides his food, he ate anything else he could chew—newspapers, paper bags, shoes, rubber boots, and erasers. When he ran out of those, he ate the edges of my curtains, the corners of my towels, the rubber heels of Luke's shoes, the handles of my pocketbooks, and the telephone cord. He even became fond of bacon and eggs and would steal our breakfast if we didn't watch him. In about three weeks, Okee's appetite for food was back to normal. He had stopped eating wood and paper things, but he never lost his fondness for rubber.

For the year that Okee was growing up I had wished for a quiet house. Now that it was still, I could not wait until Okee made it noisy again. I missed his pranks, for I knew they were a sign that he was happy and healthy. Each day I waited for some mischief, but for weeks there was none.

Then one day it happened. We left Okee alone in the bathroom for several hours. I was sure that was the safest place in the house to leave him. He had been so good for such a long time I never expected him to be naughty that day.

When I walked into the bathroom, I could not help laughing at what I saw. And I could not be the least bit angry at the mess he had made. There he was swimming merrily in the toilet tank. He had pushed off the lid and had slid down inside. The water was running furiously, for Okee had chewed up the rubber ball that was meant to stop it. The rest of the bathroom looked as if a giant windstorm had blown through. Blue toilet tissue was everywhere. The contents of the medicine cabinet were strewn all over the floor. Okee had chewed the rubber tops off the eyedroppers, made splinters out of my cotton swab sticks, and removed all the pills from their boxes. There were pills in the drinking glass, pills in the bathtub, pills in the sink, and pills in the hamper. As a final touch, Okee had pushed the button on a can of Luke's shaving lather. Shaving lather dripped from the walls and the mirror like so much whipped cream. There was no question in my mind now that Okee was well enough to be moved back to his basement room.

Day by day Okee grew stronger, but it was two months before he was completely well. Okee's recovery was remarkable, but he had not done it all by himself. It was Dr. North's skill and knowledge, more than anything else, that made this chapter in Okee's life end happily.

14

Three years have passed since the illness that almost took Okee's life. There have been other illnesses, colds, virus infections, stomach ache, a toothache from a broken tooth, but Okee did not get distemper again. To keep healthy, Okee receives several shots of vaccine serum each year. Because he lived, other otters in zoos can be given the same treatment. Now they too will have a chance to live.

Okee did not stop growing at age two as the pet-shop owner said he would. At two he weighed thirty-five pounds, at three he weighed forty-five pounds, and at four he weighed fifty pounds. When he finally stopped growing, he weighed fifty-two pounds, only two pounds less than Susie, the Giant Brazilian otter who lives at the Bronx Zoo.

The man at the pet shop didn't think Okee would grow any longer than thirty-six or forty inches, but Okee fooled him. He grew to be fifty-two inches from the tip of his nose to the tip of his tail. Okee wasn't supposed to be a giant otter, but he certainly does look like one.

Okee was now too large to swim comfortably in the bathtub, so Luke decided to build a special tank in the basement just for Okee to swim in. The tank is eight feet long, two feet wide, and two and a half feet deep— much bigger than any fish tank I have ever seen. Three of its sides are made of wood, and the front is made of thick polished plate glass. The glass alone weighs one hundred and sixty pounds. The whole tank was so heavy it took six strong men to put it in place. Before Okee was allowed to swim in it, the tank was painted with a special nontoxic paint so that Okee would not get sick if flecks of paint came off in the water. The tank was

Luke's masterpiece and he is very proud of it.

How Okee loved it! When left alone during the day, he would spend four or five hours swimming and playing in it. There was a funny game he liked to play. He would kick himself in the head with his hind foot, then he would attack his foot for having kicked him, all the while growling and screaming and churning up the water as if he were having a terrible fight. The noise was awful, but after a while we grew used to it. Now we don't bother to cover our ears when Okee is playing in the tank.

Okee grew so large and strong that we could no longer use girls as otter-sitters. The job of head otter-sitter fell to George, a rugged, husky boy of seventeen. Okee fell in love with George at once, and almost every night they would wrestle and roll and tumble on the living-room floor. George didn't seem to mind the bruises Okee gave him, and Okee didn't seem to mind the bumps on the head he got when George flipped him.

When George went away on vacation for a week, Okee did not smile the whole time

George was gone. For hours each day Okee would peer out the doors and windows hoping to see his friend come up the walk. When George finally came, Okee bubbled over with joy. He wrapped his paws around George's neck, chattered excitedly in his ear, and smothered him with wet otter kisses.

It didn't take long for word to get around that we owned an unusual but friendly pet, and Okee was invited to visit schools, libraries, and clubs all over New Jersey. Okee went to hospitals and made sick children laugh. He went to fairs and appeared on television. He even went to parties. And wherever he went, children loved him.

Okee loved performing for children. He could hardly wait to climb up on a stage and dive into his portable tank. We never trained Okee to do tricks. We didn't need to. He made up his own tricks. When Okee was sure the audience was watching, he would roll over and over and chase his tail under water. Showing off was something he did very well. If we filled his tank with inflated balloons, he would jump on them, and one by one he would pop them with his teeth. The more the children laughed, the faster Okee would pop the balloons. Soon he would have them going off like fireworks on the Fourth of July. Sometimes Okee would pop the big balloons under water. When they broke, the escaping air would shoot a stream of water straight up like a fountain.

Okee's fame traveled beyond New Jersey. A high school in the Otter Valley in Vermont adopted him as its mascot. Most of the students had never seen a live otter, for wild otters no longer live in that valley, so I was asked for pictures of Okee for the school yearbook. Then Okee was invited to the school for a special assembly in his honor. We had been thinking for some time of taking Okee on a long trip. What could be nicer than a trip to Vermont in the spring?

The distance from new Jersey to Vermont is almost 600 miles. It was too long a trip for Okee to make in one day, so we stopped overnight at a motel. The motel owner was very nice and let Okee swim in the fountain pool on the lawn. When we told him Okee would be very unhappy locked in the car all night, he said we might take Okee in the room with us. After all, it's not every motel that can boast it has had an otter as an overnight guest.

Okee wasn't very happy about being away from home, though. We tried everything we could think of to comfort him, toys, a walk, a swim, but nothing worked. As a last resort I put him in the bathtub with the water running. That did it. As long as he could splash and play under the faucet he was quiet. But as soon as I turned off the water he would cry. I wondered if the people in the room next to ours thought we were taking showers all night long.

Okee put on a fine performance for the high-school students. They were so pleased they gave him two gifts. One was a copy of the yearbook with nine photographs of him in it. The other gift was even more special. It was a handsome high-school diploma with his name lettered on it. The diploma said that Okee was an honorary member of the graduating class of 1965, and it was signed by the high-school principal and the class president. Okee is probably the only otter in the world who ever graduated from high school.

Like all otters, Okee enjoys playing in anything gooey: mud, ice cream, paste. As long as it is slippery enough for him to slide through, it is fun. One day as I watched Okee sliding across the basement floor through a puddle of spilled pancake syrup, I wondered what Okee would do if I gave him finger paint to play with. Certainly it was slippery enough to please any otter. If I was careful to give him the kind little children use in school, it wouldn't hurt him if he licked it off his paws.

I had hardly finished putting the paint and water on the paper when Okee came over to investigate. First he sniffed the paint. It didn't smell bad, so he stuck a paw in a big blob of it. It felt wonderful, so he spread it around a bit. Then he tried licking it with his tongue. It didn't taste bad either, so he put his whole face down into the paint and pushed it around with his nose. The paint must have felt like mud, for soon he was rolling and sliding through it. Each time he touched the paint with his paw, his tail, his nose, or his whiskers, he made a pretty design on the paper. When he was finished playing, he had produced, quite by accident of course, a lovely picture.

Before long, people heard about Okee's

paintings and came to see them. Some people liked the pictures so much they wanted to buy them. Newspapers all over the country carried stories about Okee, the "Ottist" and his "Ot" art. Then a lady in a big department store in New York City heard about Okee and asked if we would bring him and all his paintings to the store. We thought it would be fun to take Okee to the big city, so we agreed.

Each day for four days Okee traveled the fifty miles to the store. He liked the special room that had been prepared for him there. In it there was a large tank for swimming, a sliding board, toys, wall-to-wall carpeting, a sofa for rolling on, and even his own private bathroom. The room was on the eighth floor, so Okee had to ride an elevator to get there. He wasn't frightened at all by the strange noises it made as it whirred its way up.

When Okee got out of the elevator, he rode on a shopping cart all the way to the rear of the store. His ride took him right through the fur department. He looked so proud! And why shouldn't he? His fur coat was by far the best because he was wearing it.

But I was the proudest of all, for Okee has

made so many people happy. He has taught young and old alike to love and appreciate one of nature's most beautiful creatures, the otter.